CHRISTLIKE DIALOGUE

Engaging in Conversations that Honor God

Jeff Rosenau

CONVERSATIONS THAT GLORIFY GOD

ChristlikeDialogue.org

Christlike Dialogue

ISBN: 978-0-9717722-4-3

Printed in the United States of America

CONTENTS

DEDICATION & ACKNOWLEDGEMENTS

I dedicate this study guide to Jesus Christ,
the only hope for the people of any nation.

"Blessed is the nation whose God is Lord..."
– Psalm 33:12

I especially thank my wonderful wife Candy for her patient,
encouraging, "iron sharpening iron" input throughout all stages of
the writing process. I thank our dear friend Michelle Bervik for her
excellent editing of the content. I also thank my niece, Courtney Van
Hagen for her talented cover design and interior layout. And lastly,
I am grateful to the faithful ministry partners, without whom this
publication would not be possible.

INTRODUCTION

I Was Part of the Problem

My journey began in 1993 as I listened to the secular media and Christian leaders quarrel over controversial issues of social and political concern. I sensed something was wrong in the way God's people were responding to people with opposing views. Was it the critical, self-righteous tone I kept hearing, or was something else causing my concern? As it wasn't immediately clear to me what the problem was, I took time out to pray, "Father, there's so much wrong in our society and with Christianity; I have no idea what You would like me to do to help, but would You show me what's wrong with our society—what's wrong with Christianity—and what You would like me to do to help?"

My sons were attending a local public high school at the time and the social issue that many of us parents were concerned about was the sex education curriculum. God began to answer my prayer by leading me to two secular organizations; one was a national organization and the other a statewide non-profit organization. The first one published public school guidelines for comprehensive sexuality education for kindergarten through twelfth grade students. I first ordered a copy of the national guidelines and spent considerable time evaluating the content. As I read through them, I grew more aware of the agenda within those guidelines and how much I opposed the use of this material in the public schools. It seemed clear to me that the guidelines promoted abortion, homosexuality, and sex as a pleasurable and acceptable activity outside of marriage. From my perspective, it appeared that these guidelines were a thirteen-year package to undermine parental authority and any God-honoring influence within the public school system. For example, consider these two teaching guidelines for five-year-olds:

> *Abortion is legal in the United States.*
> *Sexual intercourse is a pleasurable activity for most adults.*

As I shared the latter quote with a teacher one day, she replied, "Well, how would you want that to read?"

I replied, "I would like it to read, 'Playing in a sandbox is a pleasurable activity for five-year-olds.' "

She smiled and said, "So would I."

The second organization, the local non-profit, trained teachers in what was referred to as Comprehensive Health Education. This group promoted or endorsed six curricula; two for elementary-age students, two for middle school, and two for high school, each having a sex education component. I picked up copies of these curricula from nearby schools, and from their main office obtained a copy of the one curriculum their organization had paid consultants to publish.

For the next several months, I researched the national guidelines and evaluated hundreds of pages of curricula that the local state organization promoted or endorsed. I found that the philosophies of these two organizations differed little, if at all.

As this research drew to completion, I recognized that some very unhealthy guidelines about sexuality were being promoted within the public schools, guidelines that came across as being unopposed to promiscuity while indifferent to the option of sexual abstinence before marriage. Believing this material to be of great concern to God, I viewed the philosophy of this national organization as the Goliath of our day and was prepared to fight, failing to remember that *our struggle is not against flesh and blood* (Ephesians 6:12).

To meet this formidable challenge, I condensed and organized my research notes to help me clearly expose agendas that I perceived to be very detrimental to young people and began meeting one-to-one with the people who helped decide what would be taught about sexuality in public school health classes. I spoke with teachers and the principal where my two sons attended high school. I went to other teachers, members of our State Board of Education, and state legislators in an effort to simply share the truth and expose what was taking place. I discovered that most of these people would listen politely as we dialogued one-to-one. A few agreed to do what they could to make changes in what was being taught.

CONVICTION

During this two-year time period, I had worked closely with nine Christian abstinence educators in Colorado. They invited me to share my research publicly with large groups of concerned citizens.

However, during those presentations I found myself to be critical and judgmental, not only of the national guidelines and state curricula, but also of the motives of the leaders within those sponsoring organizations, people whom I had never met. Gently, the Holy Spirit convicted me that the critical attitude I was conveying to the audience, was not the approach that God desired. Shortly thereafter, I had occasion to meet with a good friend and one of my mentors, Don Reeverts, president of the Denver Leadership Foundation. I would meet with Don occasionally to discuss my efforts at trying to bring about some God-honoring changes in sex education within the public schools. While Don wasn't opposed to what I was trying to accomplish, he expressed concern about how I was going about it and one day he conveyed his feelings to me with the comment, "All you want to do is fight."

On my drive home from Don's office, I thought to myself, **"Is that all I want to do is fight?"** My first thought was, "Yes, truth is worth fighting for." To further justify my behavior, my mind went back to the Old Testament because I knew there was a lot of fighting back then. But God brought me back to the New Testament and challenged me with two questions. The first was, "Do you want to follow my Son?" to which I quickly replied, "Yes, I do." The second was, "Did my Son fight and quarrel?" Then the Holy Spirit began to reveal the following passages of Scripture to me:

> **"Here is my servant whom I have chosen, the one I love, in whom I delight; I will put my Spirit on him, and he will proclaim justice to the nations. He will not quarrel..." (Matthew 12:18-19).**

> **"And the Lord's servant must not quarrel; instead, he must be kind to everyone, able to teach, not resentful. Those who oppose him he must gently instruct, in the hope that God will grant them repentance leading them to a knowledge of the truth, and that they will come to their senses and escape from the trap of the devil, who has taken them captive to do his will" (2 Timothy 2:24-26).**

> **"Instead, speaking the truth in love, we will in all things grow up into him who is the Head, that is, Christ" (Ephesians 4:15).**

GOD ANSWERS MY PRAYER

God was speaking to me and I got the message that I was not addressing the concerns over sex education in the public schools in a way that was pleasing and honoring to Him. The next morning I called the executive director of the state organization that trained teachers for comprehensive health education, and asked if she would be willing to meet with me to dialogue. I explained that my purpose was simply to see if we could find some common ground, and learn together where we clearly disagreed. Though she knew who I was and that I had been informing teachers, principals, the state legislature, and concerned citizens about the unhealthy aspects of the curricula her organization was promoting, she graciously accepted my offer.

At our first meeting, we agreed that our common ground would be healthier kids and a healthier society. We further agreed to meet and dialogue about the one curriculum their organization paid to have published. We ended up dialoguing for about two hours every month for a year. Each time, we gave each other the freedom to share the truth as we each perceived it. I would listen as she shared her perspective. Then she would listen as I pointed out and explained why I believed certain words, sentences, or phrases were not healthy for children.

At the end of that one-year period, she met with her board of directors, and they agreed to rewrite the curriculum. Although we still didn't agree in many ways, she was willing to make significant revisions. They added an entire chapter on abstinence, stating that it is a wise and desirable choice for young people, and included ten great reasons for kids to choose abstinence.

I praise God for her willingness to modify the material, as I knew that that curriculum was already being taught in more than fifty school districts in Colorado. If students had the opportunity to hear the truth about abstinence in the new chapter, they could be less at risk and better equipped to make a wise and healthy choice.

Remember my prayer? "What's wrong with our society and with Christianity?" Well, part of the answer came at the conclusion of our second dialogue. Keep in mind, this woman had worked with the public for twenty-two years. She said:

> *I want you to know that in all the years I've been doing this, this is the first time I've been able to sit down with someone who has an opposing view and have honest communication.*

God had shown me the need for Christlike dialogue. In the process, this public servant and I built a friendship and mutual respect for one another. Ironically, I had asked God to show me something that was a problem in society and with Christianity, and in the end God helped me realize, **I was part of the problem**. Here I was, a forgiven child of God, being angry and critical of people who were no worse and no more deceived than I, apart from the amazing grace that I've received from God. Although I initially had no compassion for them in my heart, God gently made it clear to me that He did—and so should I. He wanted them to experience His love through me.

With these revelations, my mindset changed completely. I began to see people through the eyes of Jesus. I felt compassion for the people God loved and wanted to set free with the truth. I thought, "How will they ever come to a knowledge of the truth if God's people don't go to them in love?"

Just think of the impact Christians can have on society if we change the way we communicate with people who see things differently than we do. Instead of speaking unkind and unloving words by way of gossip, quarreling, and argumentative debates, we can engage the culture in conversations that honor God. Through the practice of Christlike dialogue, Christians mature in Christ and represent Jesus well. As a result, more people come to know Jesus for who He truly is.

CHAPTER 1

JESUS DIDN'T DIE FOR US TO REMAIN THE SAME

For I am afraid that when I come I might not find you as I want you to be, and you might not find me as you want me to be. I fear that there may be quarreling, jealousy, outbursts of anger, factions, slander, gossip, arrogance and disorder.

– 2 Corinthians 12:20

God's will is that we would bear a family resemblance to His Son.* In other words, God's plan is for us to become more and more like Jesus—not physically, of course, but in the way we think and act and treat other people. From all eternity, the Bible says, God's plan was for us "to be conformed to the likeness of his Son" (Romans 8:29). We are part of His family—and because of that, we should bear His likeness!

Do you want to know what God's will is for you? *It is for you to become more and more like Christ.* This is spiritual maturity, and if you make this your goal, it will change your life.

—Billy Graham, *The Journey*, pp. 78-79

WE REPRESENT JESUS

As Christians, we do represent Jesus (2 Corinthians 5:20). We either represent Him well, or we represent Him poorly. Are God's children representing Jesus well when responding to people who see things differently than we do? To discover the answer, I've posed this question to many Christian audiences:

"Out of the following forms of communication, which is most prevalent among God's people:

- Gossip
- Quarreling
- Stereotyping
- Apathy
- *Christlike Dialogue?*"

More than 95 percent of every audience acknowledged that gossip, quarreling, stereotyping, and apathy are more prevalent among God's people than Christlike dialogue.

ARE WE MATURING IN CHRIST?

The Apostle Paul was aware of the spiritual immaturity of the Christian church in the city of Corinth. It had conformed to the surrounding culture evident by its worldly selfish behaviors. The Christian church was not representing Jesus well. Out of love for the people of that congregation, Paul rebuked them with these words of truth:

> **"Brothers, I could not address you as spiritual but as worldly–mere infants in Christ. I gave you milk, not solid food, for you were not yet ready for it. Indeed, you are still not ready. You are still worldly. For since there is jealousy and quarreling among you, are you not worldly? Are you not acting like mere men?" (1 Corinthians 3:1-3).**

God's desire has always been for His children to be uniquely different from the culture around us, wanting us to speak and act in ways that would represent Jesus as He truly is. But just like the Corinthians, we too miss the mark when we gossip, quarrel, and speak unkind and unloving words to others. If we are to become the people God desires us to be, how might our words change? A great place to begin, is by putting the following words into practice:

> **"Do not let any unwholesome talk come out of your mouths, but only what is helpful for building others up according to their needs, that it may benefit those who listen" (Ephesians 4:29).**

Is gossip wholesome talk? Does it build others up, or tear them down? How about quarreling?

The following new command from Jesus, if obeyed, will establish the defining characteristic of God's people, and set us apart from a secular world:

"…Love one another. As I have loved you, so you must love one another. By this all men will know that you are my disciples, if you love one another" (John 13:34-35).

Are we known by our love for one another, or is unwholesome talk still coming out of our mouths? And what about stereotyping others? Here are a few examples of the words Christians might speak when we have an unjustifiable mental picture of a group of people based solely upon their race, religion, or political viewpoint:

- An evangelical Christian says Catholics are not Christians because they teach that salvation is "earned" through good works.
- A Catholic says that Protestants will go to hell if they don't become Roman Catholics because the Catholic Church is the one true church.
- A white Christian criticizes all people of color for having bitterness and resentment toward all white people.
- An African American Christian labels all white Christians as privileged and racists.
- A liberal Christian makes it clear that she thinks all conservative Christians are deceived and more interested in a relationship with Jesus than in social justice.
- A conservative Christian makes it known that he believes all liberal Christians are blind to sin and have no deep personal relationship with Jesus.
- A Christian Republican informs her constituents that she believes all Democrats are Socialists who don't value what God values.
- A Christian Democrat makes the comment that all Republicans favor the rich and ignore the poor.

"You, my brothers, were called to be free. But do not use your freedom to indulge the sinful nature; rather, serve one another in love. The entire law is summed up in a single command: 'Love your neighbor as yourself.' If you keep on biting and devouring each other, watch out or you will be destroyed by each other" (Galatians 5:13-15).

How would anyone know how a person thinks or what they believe, and why they believe the way they do, without asking them and then really listening closely to truly understand their answers?

More importantly, did you hear any wholesome words in the above list that reflect maturity in Christ, or did their words reveal how gossip and stereotyping, rather than *dialogue*, prevent us from having the kind of conversations that draw people to Jesus Christ?

In addition to the absence of words that build others up, did you notice what else was missing? *Love and dialogue.* When that occurs, we are left representing Jesus poorly as we communicate according to our old sinful nature.

How easily we forget we have been graciously forgiven by God, and that He wants us to extend that same grace to others, without compromising truth.

I believe the clear, profound, and timely exhortation from our heavenly Father to us, His children, is this:

It's time to grow up, into the likeness of My Son.

Why? Because gossip and stereotyping – quarreling and argumentative monologues – unkind and unloving words, grieve the heart of God. They require no transformation. When we communicate in these ways we remain mere infants in Christ, and continue to misrepresent the character of Jesus. So let's remind ourselves and each other that **Jesus didn't die for us to remain the same**.

My prayer and hope is that this study produces growth in our knowledge of the Son of God so that our abiding relationship with Him enables us to represent Jesus well to people with differing views.

In Matthew 12:34b, Jesus said, *For out of the overflow of the heart the mouth speaks.* If the words we speak require change, we must first examine our hearts. Do we long for things the world offers and values, or is it our heart's desire to become more and more like Christ, valuing what God values?

As you read, you'll discover that this book is a lot less about learning how to communicate, and a lot more about getting to know Jesus as He truly is. Rather than presenting a "how to" book or a "steps to follow" manual, this book offers readers opportunities to consider what it means to follow Jesus Christ and become more like Him through the words we speak. In so doing, we see God using us to engage others with differing views in ways we never imagined!

GOSSIP AND STEREOTYPING

– quarreling and argumentative monologues –
unkind and unloving words,

GRIEVE THE HEART OF GOD.

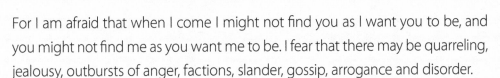

For I am afraid that when I come I might not find you as I want you to be, and you might not find me as you want me to be. I fear that there may be quarreling, jealousy, outbursts of anger, factions, slander, gossip, arrogance and disorder.

– 2 Corinthians 12:20

DISCUSSION QUESTIONS
CHAPTER 1

Jesus Didn't Die For Us to Remain the Same

1. Read Ephesians 4:22-24. Jesus didn't die and rise again for us to remain the same, but Christians are remaining the same when we continue to gossip, quarrel, speak unkind and unloving words to others, or on the other hand, remain apathetic because we fear offending people. What will it take for Christians to replace natural, worldly responses with conversations that honor God?

2. Read and meditate on Luke 6:45, Ephesians 4:13-15 and James 3:2. Why are the words you speak, and the words you refrain from speaking so important to God?

3. How might responding to people with differing views by gossiping, quarreling, debating, or avoiding them, keep us from maturing in Christ?

4. How might these kinds of responses affect their view of Christ and hinder you from having a spiritual impact in their lives?

5. Which of these is hardest for you to avoid? Gossiping, quarreling, getting into a heated debate, or responding with sarcasm or in another unkind way? Or are you someone who lacks interest and avoids discussing important issues all together? List the situations, issues, and/or people that are most likely to provoke you to respond in a negative way.

GUIDELINE FOCUS: **PRAY**

ASK GOD TO HELP YOU GAIN A GREATER UNDERSTANDING OF EACH OTHER, OF WHAT IS TRUE, AND OF WHAT GOD MIGHT WANT TO REVEAL ABOUT HIMSELF THROUGH THE CONVERSATION.

See Appendix A on page 130 for a list of the Guidelines for *Christlike Dialogue*. Each week of this study, you are asked to focus on one of the guidelines for a Christlike dialogue. The guidelines are not a list of steps to follow but rather biblical truths to consider when preparing your own heart to engage in dialogue in a Christlike manner.

First read the guideline. Then write out the accompanying Scripture reference in the space provided in the Journal you will find in Appendix B. Repetitively read the accompanying Scripture reference, committing it to memory if possible. This week's focus is on the first guideline; PRAY. Look up Psalm 18:30, and copy it into your Journal in Appendix B on page 131.

Spend some time in your group praying for one another about at least one of the difficult situations or relationships each member has listed in question 5. Your prayer time might include asking God to:

- Reveal what He might want you to learn through one of these difficult situations or relationships.
- Be your shield and your strength as you engage in Christlike dialogue with difficult or challenging people or situations in the weeks ahead.
- Help you to more deeply and personally know Jesus as the way, the truth and the life.

....

APPLICATION

Look up and write out Psalm 19:14 on page 131 in the Journal found in Appendix B and place a copy where you will see it all week, perhaps on the bathroom mirror, on your car's visor, or on your screen saver. Memorize this verse.

Over the next week keep a daily log and write down each time you gossip, quarrel, debate, and/or say any unkind or unloving words to anyone else, even if it is the driver cutting you off in traffic! See Appendix B on pages 131-134 for a Weekly Log provided for you to complete. Prior to your next small group meeting review this log and your answers to question 5 and be prepared to discuss with your small group.

If there is a person in your life with whom you currently have a difference of opinion, I encourage you to pray and ask God if it is His will for you to initiate dialogue with that person. If you have peace that it is, ask God for His wisdom, blessing, and timing before you proceed to initiate dialogue, and be sure to invite the Holy Spirit to join you in the conversation.

CHAPTER 2

SEIZE THE OPPORTUNITY

Do not conform any longer to the pattern of this world, but be transformed by the renewing of your mind. Then you will be able to test and approve what God's will is – his good, pleasing and perfect will.

– Romans 12:2

What was Christ's relationship to the Spirit? Again, one of utter dependence. Nowhere do we read that Jesus performed any miracles or uttered marvelous teachings before His baptism and filling by the Spirit.

That simple dependence upon the Holy Spirit was necessary on Jesus' part for the accomplishing of God's will through Him. It is also necessary on my part if I am to accomplish God's will through me.

—W. Glyn Evans, *Daily with my Lord*, August 20

If Jesus didn't die for us to remain the same, what needs to change? We do. Rather than remain part of the problem, we should seize the opportunity to become part of the solution. Instead of being conformed to this world, we can be transformed by the Holy Spirit and become the people God is calling us to be. We have a choice. We can conform to this world and join in all the argumentative monologues, name calling, animosity, bitterness, hatred and division. Or, we can choose to allow the Holy Spirit to transform our lives so we can respond to opposition humbly, respectfully, with grace, and without compromising truth.

It has always been God's will for His people to be uniquely different from the world around us. He wants us to represent Jesus well so others will be drawn to Him. Disagreements and conflict provide great opportunity for Christians to have that kind of observable difference. **Will we seize the opportunity?**

What does this kind of transformation look like? In the chart below, the apostles Peter and Paul respond to people of opposing views. First, they have a natural (worldly) response. After being filled with the Holy Spirit, they learned to respond in Christlike ways.

	NATURAL RESPONSE (WORLDLY)	UNNATURAL RESPONSE (SPIRITUAL - CHRISTLIKE)
PETER	The soldiers and officials have come to arrest Jesus. What is Peter's response? He cuts off the ear of the high priest's servant (See John 18:1-11). What was Jesus' response to Peter? He rebuked Him (v.11). Why? Peter was getting in the way of God's will being done.	After being filled with and transformed by the Holy Spirit, Peter wrote: *Do not repay evil with evil or insult with insult, but with blessing… (1 Peter 3:9).* *But in your hearts set apart Christ as Lord. Always be prepared to give an answer to everyone who asks you to give the reason for the hope that you have. But do this with gentleness and respect… (1 Peter 3:15).*
PAUL	Before Jesus confronts Paul on the road to Damascus, Paul was opposed to Christians. His response was to imprison and beat those who believed in Jesus. And he gave his approval to those who stoned Stephen to death (See Acts 22:19-20). Why did Jesus rebuke Paul? Paul was getting in the way of God's will being done.	After being filled with and transformed by the Holy Spirit, Paul wrote: *Get rid of all bitterness, rage and anger, brawling and slander, along with every form of malice. Be kind and compassionate to one another, forgiving each other, just as in Christ God forgave you (Ephesians 4:31-32).*

Rather than remain part of the problem, we should
SEIZE THE OPPORTUNITY TO BECOME PART OF THE SOLUTION.

As the spiritual battle between good and evil intensifies, the need for spiritual maturity among God's people will be great. If we too are to avoid getting in the way of God's will being done, it is essential for Christians to be prepared to represent Jesus well in the face of persecution.

We mature spiritually as we *live by* and are *filled with the Spirit, rather than gratifying the desires of our sinful nature* (Galatians 5:16; Ephesians 5:18). This means that throughout each day we choose to walk in the light of the Spirit's presence within us, allowing the mind of Christ to replace the thoughts of our old sinful nature.

That old nature provokes us to respond to people of opposing views with *hatred, discord, jealousy, fits of rage, selfish ambition, dissentions, factions and envy* (Galatians 5:20-21). But when we choose to keep in step with the Holy Spirit, our new life in Christ becomes evident as our responses then convey the fruit of the Spirit: *love, joy, peace, patience, kindness, goodness, faithfulness, gentleness and self-control* (Galatians 5:22-23).

Most of us are at risk of responding in the flesh (our old sinful nature), rather than in the Spirit of Christ (our new nature) to people who keep us from getting our way, or those who become a hindrance to our lives going smoothly. Humanly speaking, it feels more satisfying to gossip or quarrel then to take the time to love someone. But we have a higher calling, and that is to **be conformed to the likeness of Christ**.

CONFLICT OFFERS OPPORTUNITY

Conflict usually evokes a response of increased anxiety, anger, and/or avoidance. These are normal natural responses to conflict. But have you ever considered that the conflicts you face may actually be opportunities to embrace?

> **"Consider it pure joy, my brothers, whenever you face trials of many kinds, because you know that the testing of your faith develops perseverance. Perseverance must finish its work so that you may be mature and complete, not lacking anything" (James 1:2-4).**

It's not natural to consider it pure joy when we face trials, including disagreements we have with other people. But if we see circumstances from a spiritual perspective, we begin to understand that when God allows people with differing views into our lives, any ensuing conflict offers us opportunity to reach our **goal of becoming more like Christ**. How, you say? By giving us opportunity to love others as Christ has loved us, including those who rub us the wrong way. It is in loving those who are hard to get along with (and perhaps that includes you and me), that we share in the sufferings of Christ as we experience how painful it can be to love someone who rejects us, or disagrees with our way of thinking, or wrongs us in some way. Do you have a controlling spouse, a rebellious teenager, or an irritating in-law in your life? Or is your opportunity with a demanding boss, grumpy neighbor, or a friend at work who is of a different race or religion? Who has God allowed into your life who sees things differently than you do? How does God want you to respond to and communicate with them in ways that convey the love of Christ?

Remember this quote from Billy Graham in chapter one:

> *Do you want to know what God's will is for you? It is for you to become more and more like Christ. This is spiritual maturity, and if you make this your goal, it will change your life.*

Our goal in life will guide our responses to people with whom we experience conflict. If our goal is to get our own way, our responses will be much different than if our goal is to communicate in a Christlike manner. As God's children, we need to remember that He is at work within us to *will and to act according to his good purpose* (Philippians 2:13), so that our character reflects His. Just like the apostles Peter and Paul, we have a choice. We can choose to respond naturally and immaturely, and remain part of the problem, or we can choose to live by the Spirit, respond in Christlike ways, and become part of the solution.

For greater understanding of the significant difference between natural (worldly) responses and unnatural (spiritual – Christlike) responses, we'll look at two conversations between an employer and an employee. The second conversation illustrates what can happen when God's people are willing to break from the worldly culture around us.

FIRST CONVERSATION: EMPLOYER AND EMPLOYEE

One party in this conversation is a middle aged female who is the owner of a successful local business. The other person is a new employee, a single mom in her late twenties who arrives to work fifteen minutes late three days in a row. In this first conversation, the employer responds in a **natural**, but **worldly** way.

1st DAY

Employer: "You're a new employee, and you get to work fifteen minutes late? Don't be late again!"

Employee: "I'm sorry, but…"

Employer: "No buts! Be on time tomorrow!"

2nd DAY

Employer: "Maybe I didn't make myself clear yesterday."

Employee: "You did make yourself clear; and I apologize again. I tried my best to be here on time, but…"

Employer: "No buts! I don't expect you to try. I expect you to be here, **on time**!"

Employee: "Yes, ma'am."

3rd DAY

Employer: "Your tardiness is unacceptable! You are fired!"

Employee: "Please don't fire me. I really need this job. If you would just give me a few minutes to explain…"

Employer: "All our employees start their work on time. It is not fair to them when you come in fifteen minutes late every day, especially as a new employee. Now clear everything out of your desk, and leave!"

SECOND CONVERSATION: EMPLOYER AND EMPLOYEE

Everything remains the same, except the employer's response. This time, she responds in an **unnatural** (spiritual – Christlike) way.

1st DAY

Employer: "I noticed you were late today. What happened?"

Employee: "I'm sorry, but I'm a single parent with a 3-year-old daughter and a 6-year-old son who I drop off at school every morning. The school has a system for cars to line up so parents can drop the kids off in an orderly way. They don't start checking kids in until fifteen minutes before I'm supposed to be at work. Although I was third in line, this morning the process was unusually slow. Of course, I realize that none of this excuses me from being late."

Employer: "I'm sure you are trying your best to be on time. Let's see how it goes tomorrow. By the way, what are your children's names?"

Employee: "Martha is the three-year old and Joshua is six. Thank you for asking."

2ND DAY

Employer: "How was the car line at school this morning?"

Employee: "I apologize again for being late. I did everything I could to be on time and left early so I could be the first car in line; but as we left home and were about a mile down the road, Joshua told me he forgot something he needed for school, so I turned back to get it."

Employer: "I understand. We have four children. They're older now, but I certainly remember some of the challenges that come with three and six-year olds. So, how did your first day at work go yesterday?"

Employee: "It was great, and thank you so much for your understanding. I will try my best to be on time tomorrow."

3RD DAY

Employer: "I noticed you arrived a little later than you had before. Please come into my office. I'd like to hear how things went for you this morning."

Employee: "First, the kids were not cooperative in getting ready this morning. Then, I had to stop and get gas because I forgot to get it yesterday on the way home. I had to hurry from work to get Josh to soccer practice last night. Because of all that, I ended up way back in the line of cars at school. I'm so sorry."

Employer: "It's really hard being a single mom, isn't it?"

Employee: "I cannot begin to tell you how awfully hard it is to assume all the responsibilities that were supposed to be shared by both my husband and myself. It wasn't supposed to be this way."

Employer: "I'd like you to join me and two other employees for lunch today. They are both single moms in their late twenties, and they each have two children about the same age as your children. Also, I would like to change your work hours so you can begin work a half hour later with the choice of working a half hour longer at the end of the day, or by taking a half hour for lunch, instead of an hour. If you think that can be of help, which would you prefer?"

Employee: "I would love to join you and the single moms for lunch, and I cannot thank you enough for the extra half hour in the morning. That will lighten my load significantly, and a half hour for lunch is plenty for me. But won't some of your employees see that as favoritism, and be offended?"

Employer: "Why don't you let me worry about that? Different employees have different needs. I like to think of our employees as part of my family and if we can meet a need, I think God likes it when we do just that. This business is His and as long as we take care of each other and our customers in an excellent way, I believe God is pleased because we keep getting more and more business and are able to employ many people in this town."

There is a life-changing difference between viewing people and circumstances as most people do, in a **natural** way from a **worldly** perspective versus seeing people from a **spiritual** perspective through the eyes of Jesus, in ways that are totally **unnatural**, yet very Christlike.

CHRISTLIKE DIALOGUE IS NOT NATURAL

Gossip, quarreling, argumentative monologues, apathy, unkind and unloving words, are all natural responses to people we view as opposition, or even as enemies. Christlike dialogue, on the other hand, involves unnatural responses.

Christlike dialogue is defined as honest conversation guided by the Holy Spirit that includes:

- Other-minded listening
- Seeking and speaking the truth in love
- Focusing on Christ's interests
- Trusting God with the outcome

In later chapters, these four characteristics of Christlike dialogue will be explained more thoroughly.

As we put Christlike dialogue into practice, we realize we can become part of the solution, rather than remain part of the problem. Instead of conforming to this world, staying immature in Christ and representing Jesus poorly by gossiping and quarreling, we can **seize the opportunity** to become more like Jesus and represent Him well through the words we speak.

In the chart that follows, you can see that Christlike dialogue is not a natural response to conflict; it's an unnatural spiritual response. That's why it's called **Christlike** dialogue.

NATURAL RESPONSE (WORLDLY)	UNNATURAL RESPONSE (SPIRITUAL - CHRISTLIKE)
Self-centered, quick to speak, slow to listen	Other-minded, quick to listen, slow to speak (Philippians 2:3-4; James 1:19-20)
Speaking what you perceive to be truth, without speaking it in love. Grace is absent.	Seeks and speaks the truth in love by humbly extending grace; asking good questions, and listening well without compromising truth in the process. (John 14:6; 8:32; Ephesians 4:15)
The focus is on self-interests. You have selfish ambition and a strong desire to be "right" and get your way. (James 3:16; 4:1-3)	The focus is on Christ's interests. (1 Timothy 1:15; Ephesians 4:13) The conflict is embraced as an opportunity to mature in Christ and represent Jesus well so others come to know Him as He truly is.
You try to control the outcome.	You speak the truth in love as you perceive it, and you trust God with the outcome. (2 Timothy 2:24-26)

Do not conform any longer to the pattern of this world, but be transformed by the renewing of your mind. Then you will be able to test and approve what God's will is – his good, pleasing and perfect will.

– Romans 12:2

DISCUSSION QUESTIONS
CHAPTER 2

Seize the Opportunity

1. When faced with conflict, how are you most likely to respond, and why is that?

2. Read Matthew 7:12 and Luke 10:25-37. In what ways does the employer in the first conversation miss the opportunity, and pass by the employee? In what ways does the employer represent Jesus well in the second conversation?

3. What are some reasons Christians should embrace conflict? How can simple disagreements, and other conflicts, become opportunities to embrace instead of something to avoid or get upset about?

4. Read the following:

A MISSED OPPORTUNITY

One day I received a telephone bill for our ministry, and noticed an error. I called the phone company, explained the mistake, and asked them to correct it. They said they would.

A month went by. I received another phone bill. The mistake had not been corrected. I called a second time. Calmly and politely I explained the error, and asked for it to be corrected. The person on the line assured me that the correction would be made.

Another month passed. The phone bill arrived without the anticipated correction. I was thinking to myself, **"Why can't these people get it right?"** I called again, and in a reasonable tone of voice explained that the error they twice said would be corrected, was still there. For the third time I was told it would be taken care of.

Thirty more days passed. And you guessed it. I got the bill, and the correction had not been made. The thought returned, **"Why can't these people get it right?"** During my next call, I responded in less than a Christlike way.

When I finished, the woman on the other end of the line asked, "Didn't you say you work for a ministry?"

Having been immediately convicted, I replied, "Yes I did, and thank you for reminding me." I apologized to the woman for getting upset, and for not responding as I should have. We then had a cordial conversation as she shared that she and her husband also have a ministry.

The next time I received our bill in the mail, the correction had been made. And then the light bulb came on. **I was the one who wasn't getting it right.** God had given me another opportunity to respond as Christ would with patience and gentleness, yet I forgot and I failed to practice what Christ had taught me. To correct this, God used a fellow believer to hold me accountable. That experience was a powerful reminder of our need to abide in Christ moment by moment so that we're never caught off guard and respond inappropriately, as I did.

Because God is gracious, He initially gives us practice through minor disagreements as I've described above. However, I believe His goal in giving us opportunities through conflict is ultimately to deepen our relationship with Him so we'll be prepared to represent Jesus well, even when more serious trials and persecution come our way.

Share similar examples you may have experienced. Did you seize the opportunity to represent Jesus well, or did you miss it? Explain your answer and the outcome of your response.

GUIDELINE FOCUS: **BE HONEST**

AUTHENTICITY IS HIGHLY VALUED.

Look up Proverbs 24:26, the verse on which this guideline is based, and copy it into your Journal in Appendix B on page 135.

APPLICATION

Spend some time in prayer and ask God to show you who you may need to approach and ask for forgiveness for any unkind and unloving words you have said that have resulted in a broken or strained relationship. Perhaps this is the person you listed in Chapter One, Discussion Question 5.

Write out a letter asking for forgiveness for specific words that have been said.

Read and meditate on Psalm 139:23-24 and Ephesians 4:29-32 to prepare your heart before engaging in conversation with that person. Pray that God would open a door for your dialogue to proceed with the person you need to forgive. Wait until you receive a clear nudging from the Holy Spirit that the time is right to initiate a Christlike dialogue to ask for forgiveness, and then **seize the opportunity**.

CHAPTER 3

OTHER-MINDED LISTENING

Do nothing out of selfish ambition or vain conceit, but in humility consider others better than yourselves. Each of you should look not only to your own interests, but also to the interests of others.

– Philippians 2:3-4

My dear brothers, take note of this: Everyone should be quick to listen, slow to speak and slow to become angry, for man's anger does not bring about the righteous life that God desires.

– James 1:19-20

WHY LISTEN?

We must regularly ask ourselves if our conversations live up to the servant attitude of Jesus. Do we take the time to understand what others are trying to tell us? Do we care enough to listen?

Listening displays the opposite of selfishness because it makes another person more important than ourselves. Any such act of humility allows the character of Jesus to grow in our lives.

It's only as we take the time to listen to people that we will begin to understand why they speak and act the way they do.

Are we willing to take that time?

Jesus did. With the Samaritan woman in the middle of the day. With Nicodemus in the middle of the night. And with us whenever we've needed to talk.

Do we really want to be like Jesus?

That's the real question, isn't it?

For if we become like Him, it will change not only the way we live; it will change the way we listen.

—John Vawter, *Uncommon Graces*, pp. 44-45, 56

FIRST CHARACTERISTIC OF CHRISTLIKE DIALOGUE:

OTHER-MINDED LISTENING

A marriage relationship gives us a great example to remind us of our need to be excellent listeners. Did you ever wonder why God designed opposites to attract and marry each other? Could it be to give us practice at becoming more other-minded and more like Christ in the process?

The Bible explains that God created male and female (Genesis 1:27). The marital conflicts that arise when spouses see things from different perspectives are discussed in the book, *Love & Respect*. In his book, Emerson Eggerich states that men have a primary need for respect from their wives, while women have a primary need for love from their husbands (See Ephesians 5:33). This reminds spouses to be aware of each other's needs, and becoming great listeners is crucial to becoming more other-minded.

Following are two conversations. The first conversation is an example of two monologues between two **self-centered** spouses who are **quick to speak**. The second is a Christlike dialogue between a husband and wife who are becoming **other-minded**, and are **quick to listen**. The conversation takes place a week before the couple's anniversary.

FIRST CONVERSATION: HUSBAND AND WIFE

In the first conversation, the husband has been busy at work and doesn't take time to consider where his wife might enjoy going for a romantic dinner. He thinks she will gladly help him choose a restaurant. As the conversation unfolds, listen closely to hear how both husband and wife fail to consider the primary needs (love and respect) of their spouse. Instead, their focus is on getting their own needs met.

Husband: "Honey, our anniversary is only a week away. I think we should go out to dinner and celebrate. Where would you like to go?"

Wife: "I don't know. Where do you think we should go?"

Husband: "I don't know. I want to take you wherever you would like to go."

Wife: "I want you to decide."

Husband: "Okay, let's go to…" (and he names his favorite restaurant).

Wife: "I don't want to go there."

Husband: "Where would you like to go?"

Wife: "I don't know. Just not there."

Husband: "Well, how will I know unless you tell me?"

Wife: "Exactly. You wouldn't know unless I told you, but I'll bet you know the favorite restaurant of your clients at work, don't you?"

Husband: "What does that have to do with us and our anniversary?"

Wife: "I think you are more in love with your work than you are with me."

Husband: "I don't have a clue what you mean. I try to be thoughtful and ask where you would like to have dinner on our anniversary, and what do I get in return? Will you ever stop nagging me about my work? At least they appreciate me at the office."

Wife: "Why wouldn't they? You're sensitive to meeting their needs."

Husband: "That's the end of this conversation. I'm done talking."

Wife: "Yeah, big surprise. Run away from the problem, like you usually do."

It's pretty clear that each spouse is focused on self rather than their partner's primary need (love or respect). Instead, they want their own needs met. In James 3:16, we learn that *where you have envy and **selfish ambition**, there you find disorder and every evil practice*. And in James 4:1-3, **self-centered** motives are identified as the cause of fights and quarrels. When either person has selfish ambition, you can expect two monologues, with an absence of communication that glorifies God. So if you find yourselves in a disagreement with someone, ask God to reveal any selfish ambition within the heart of either person prior to discussing differences.

When either person has

SELFISH AMBITION,

you can expect two monologues, with an absence of

COMMUNICATION THAT GLORIFIES GOD.

SECOND CONVERSATION: HUSBAND AND WIFE

The second conversation is a Christlike dialogue between the husband and wife, who are now becoming other-minded, and are closely listening to each other in order to understand and meet each other's needs. When we focus on the other person, we listen to discern what need or needs of theirs are not being met. Other-minded listening takes the focus off of me and puts it on how I can best love the other person with the love of Christ, seen in the following Christlike dialogue.

Husband: "I began our conversation by asking you where you would like to go for dinner to celebrate our anniversary because I love you. Why did that offend you?"

Wife: "My thought was, if you loved me, you would know what restaurant I enjoy the most. I know you well enough to know that the restaurant you suggested is your favorite, rather than mine."

Husband: "That's true. That was pretty inconsiderate of me. Sadly, after you made the comment about me knowing the favorite restaurant of my clients, I realized you were correct. But do you see how your statement that I'm more in love with my work than with you came across to me as being disrespectful?"

Wife: "I didn't intend to be disrespectful. I was just hurt that you couldn't remember my favorite restaurant and I guess I just wanted to hurt you in return, and that was pretty disrespectful of me."

Husband: "I'm beginning to understand that I've been a crummy lover, but not because I don't love you. I love you very much. The problem has been that I've focused so much energy on getting **my need for respect** met through work, that I've neglected **your need to be loved**. Will you forgive me?"

Wife: "I do forgive you, and I've let you down in a similar way. I've been so focused on all the ways that I don't feel loved by you that I have not been respecting you for the man you are, your character, and the way you approach things. I've failed miserably at meeting your need for respect, again! But it has never been because I don't respect you. I do respect you; you know that, but I haven't communicated that to you in a while. Will you forgive me?"

Husband: "I do forgive you, Honey, but help me understand what love looks like to you."

Wife: "You love me well in many ways, like taking time to talk with me right now in a gentle, kind way. You know I like a good morning kiss and hate it when you are rushed and forget. I really want us to have a date night once a week and I know you have been too busy with work, but it is really important to me to have your undivided attention so you can just listen to me and not try to give me the quick fix solution for what's going on with the kids and daily life challenges. Also, words of appreciation mean a lot to me."

Wife: "Will you help me understand what respect looks like to you?"

Husband: "Sure. This verse pops into mind: *A gentle and quiet spirit, which is of great worth in God's sight* (1 Peter 3:4). That doesn't mean I don't welcome your opinion; it just means your opinion is given in a respectful way just as you would want me to do with you. No nagging. It's fine to bring up something that needs fixing or something else that you would like me to do, but I ask you to be patient. Other ways I feel your respect is when you express interest in the work I'm doing, and I love to hear words of encouragement from you."

Wife: "My desire is to respect you in ways that are pleasing and honoring to God, so when I'm disrespectful, will you please let me know?

Husband: "I will. Let's pray. Father, we love you and we desire to be obedient to you. I ask for your grace and wisdom to love my wife in all the ways you want me to love her."

Wife: "Father, I ask for your grace and discernment to know how to show respect for my husband in all the ways You desire me to."

Husband: "Father, we ask for your blessing upon our marriage. May it be a marriage that is pleasing and honoring to you, and a great example for our children."

REPLACING THE OLD WITH THE NEW

Self-centeredness and being quick to speak result in quarrels, fighting, and disorder. They represent our old nature. **Selfish ambition usually leads to two monologues, while other-minded listening initiates Christlike dialogue.** Being other-minded and quick to listen reflect our new life in Jesus Christ.

If we are to represent Jesus well through the words we speak, our hearts must be cleansed of all selfish ambition so that the other-minded life of Christ shines through us. It begins by choosing to become an **other-minded listener**.

Do nothing out of selfish ambition or vain conceit, but in humility consider others better than yourselves. Each of you should look not only to your own interests, but also to the interests of others.

– Philippians 2:3-4

My dear brothers, take note of this: Everyone should be quick to listen, slow to speak and slow to become angry, for man's anger does not bring about the righteous life that God desires.

– James 1:19-20

DISCUSSION QUESTIONS
CHAPTER 3

Other-Minded Listening

1. The conversations involved a married couple, but the principle of being an other-minded listener applies to any conversation you might have. Think about what it feels like to truly be listened to by someone; then list the qualities of an effective other-minded listener.

2. Review the list of qualities from question 1 and discuss with your group which of these is most challenging for you to put into practice. Copy your group's list of qualities of effective listening onto the Journal in Appendix B on page 136.

3. In what ways is listening an expression of love and/or respect?

4. Read James 3:16; 4:1-3. List some examples of selfish ambition that God has revealed to you in your own life or in the lives of others. Share with your group how selfish ambition may be keeping you from maturing in Christ and representing Jesus well?

GUIDELINE FOCUS: **LISTEN**

LEARN FROM ONE ANOTHER AND DON'T ATTEMPT TO PERSUADE OTHERS TO YOUR POINT OF VIEW OR ASSUME SOMEONE IS WRONG JUST BECAUSE HE OR SHE DOESN'T AGREE WITH YOU. SEEK TO UNDERSTAND AND BE UNDERSTOOD AS TO WHY EACH OF YOU BELIEVE WHAT YOU BELIEVE.

Look up James 1:19-20, Philippians 2:3-4, the two verses on which this guideline is based and copy them into your Journal in Appendix B on page 136.

APPLICATION

Ask someone in your small group or a family member or friend to spend 15 minutes of face to face time with you so you can practice becoming an other-minded listener. Prepare three or four open ended questions. Listen closely to the answers to each question without interjecting your opinion or interrupting other than to ask for clarification. Listen closely to the answers. Do maintain eye contact; observe the other person's body language and tone of voice; and do not take notes or engage in any other activity while listening. When they have finished answering as many questions as time allows, tell them what you heard them say in each response and ask for feedback on how well you listened and/or understood what was being said. Share with your group what was hard or easy for you and what you learned from this exercise. Here are some examples of questions you can use:

- If you could have any occupation, what would it be, and why?
- What is your greatest concern about America, and why?
- What is your purpose for being here on earth?
- What role does Jesus have in your life?

For more examples of questions, see Garry Poole's book, *The Complete Book of Questions: 1001 Conversation Starters for Any Occasion.* (Poole, 2003)

CHAPTER 4

SEEK AND SPEAK
THE TRUTH IN LOVE

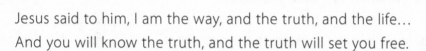

Jesus said to him, I am the way, and the truth, and the life…
And you will know the truth, and the truth will set you free.

— John 14:6; 8:32 ESV

Instead, speaking the truth in love, we will in all things grow up into him who is the Head, that is, Christ.

— Ephesians 4:15

God is at work taking people who instinctively speak for themselves and transforming them into people who effectively speak for him.

Paul Tripp, *War of Words*, p. 7

SEEK AND SPEAK THE TRUTH IN LOVE

The effect of speaking the truth in love is that we will in all things grow up into Christ. In other words, if we learn to speak the truth **in love**, we will represent Jesus well and others will be drawn to Him. For this transformation to occur, Christ's interests will replace selfish ambition; and we will become more other-minded and available to listen to people to whom God leads us. We will in fact be engaged in fulfilling the great commission as explained in **Matthew 28:19-20**:

> **"Therefore go and make disciples of all nations, baptizing them in the name of the Father and of the Son and of the Holy Spirit, and teaching them to obey everything I have commanded you. And surely I am with you always, to the very end of the age."**

If we are to make disciples, we must teach them to obey Christ's command to love one another as Jesus has loved us (John 13:34-35). With this new mindset, we will begin to see conflict, even simple disagreements, as opportunities for God to conform us to the likeness of His Son. We will learn to love people, even those who seem "unlovable," and through us God can draw them to Himself. Our motivation for dialogue will change from a desire to be "right" and persuade people to see things exactly as we do, to love and concern for the salvation of the lost and the sanctification of the saved. Instead of focusing on a divisive issue or concern, we can focus more on our relationship with the person we are engaging in conversation. We find ways to express the love of Christ to someone in desperate need of the truth that Jesus loves them and desires a relationship with them. How very sad it is when well intentioned Christians self-righteously speak about issues and topics in unloving, harsh, and judgmental ways that push people away from Christ instead of drawing them to Him.

Through the following conversations, we can experience the difference it makes when we change our motive, and focus on speaking the truth in love; with grace appropriate to the situation.

FIRST CONVERSATION: PREGNANT TEEN AND TEACHER

Let's set the stage. One of the participants in this conversation is a sixteen-year-old girl named Mary who is pregnant. She is not a Christian. Her boyfriend refuses to support her financially. Her parents are very upset and express their disappointment by refusing to help their daughter in any way. Distraught, and now contemplating abortion, Mary decides to first confide in one of her teachers, a woman who is a Christian.

The other participant in this conversation is the teacher, an **immature** Christian who believes it's her duty to convince this girl of the truth that abortion is a sin and not to be considered as an option. The focus is on the **issue** of abortion!

As they meet, the first conversation goes like this:

Mary: "I just found out that I'm pregnant, and I need to talk with someone about it. I'm scared and don't know what to do."

Teacher: "What do you mean you don't know what to do? You should have the baby."

Mary: "It's not that simple. My boyfriend doesn't want to marry me. My parents are very upset and unwilling to help me financially. I'm considering an abortion."

Teacher: "I don't think you should have an abortion."

Mary: "Well, what other options do I have?"

Teacher: "You should have the baby. Maybe your boyfriend will change his mind. If not, you can always put the baby up for adoption."

Mary: "I can't do that. Babies cost money and I don't have any. My parents won't give me a dime. I see abortion as my only option. I believe it's what's best for me, under the circumstances."

Teacher: "Don't you realize that you would be taking the life of an innocent unborn baby?"

Mary: "It's not a baby yet. I don't care what you taught us in class, there's plenty of information on line that says it's nothing more than tissue."

HOW VERY SAD IT IS WHEN WELL INTENTIONED CHRISTIANS, **self-righteously speak about issues and topics in unloving, harsh, and judgmental ways that** PUSH PEOPLE AWAY FROM CHRIST INSTEAD OF DRAWING THEM TO HIM.

Teacher: "That's not true. Listen to what the Bible says in Psalm 139:13-16."

Mary: "Why would I care what the Bible says. God doesn't care about me. If He did, I wouldn't be in this mess."

Teacher: "Don't blame God. You and your boyfriend should not have had sex until you were married. Don't you know what the Bible says about sexual immorality?"

Mary: "Hey, I came to you because you call yourself a 'Christian.' I thought you might be able to help me. But I'm sorry I did. You can save your preachin' for someone else."

In the first conversation, the teacher was focused on the **issue** of abortion. Her motive was to persuade Mary to her point of view regarding abortion. In the process, the teacher lost sight of the importance of the **relationship** and Mary's need for grace and compassion. Although truth was spoken, it was not spoken in love.

CHANGE OF FOCUS AND MOTIVE

Regardless of what the issue may be in any disagreement, you will be faced with two choices:

1. Will you focus on the **issue**, or will you focus on the **relationship**?

2. Will you have a motive to **be "right" and to persuade someone to your point of view**, or will you choose a motive of **love for God and love for the other person**?

The second conversation is between the same two people, but this time it is a Christlike dialogue. In this conversation, we learn how to **effectively speak as *Christ's ambassadors*** (2 Corinthians 5:20). The focus now shifts to the relationship rather than the issue, and the motive is to love this girl with the love of Christ, and in this way, **speak the truth in love**.

SECOND CONVERSATION: PREGNANT TEEN AND TEACHER

The pregnant girl's circumstances have not changed. There is, however, a noticeable change in the Christian—she has been growing in Christ and has asked Him to teach her how to love those with whom she disagrees. Because of this change of heart, her response is quite different from what it has been.

During this dialogue, the Christian's focus is on building a relationship with Mary, rather than on persuading her not to abort her baby. The desire to control has been replaced with love for this young girl. Seeing more clearly from God's perspective, the teacher now views Mary, not as opposition, but as a fellow human being who is hurting and in need of compassion. The teacher becomes empathetic, trying to imagine what it would be like to be sixteen and pregnant, rejected by a boyfriend and parents, and left feeling unwanted, unloved, scared, and all alone. She asks herself, "If I were in her shoes, how would I want someone to treat me?"

In this conversation, listen closely to identify ways in which the teacher now demonstrates **maturity in Christ**.

Mary: "I just found out that I'm pregnant, and I need to talk with someone. I'm scared and don't know what to do."

Teacher: "How can I help?"

Mary: "Well, my boyfriend doesn't talk to me anymore. He won't even return my texts. My parents are really upset. They told me not to expect any help from them. But my friend, Heather, says she knows where I can have an abortion. I'm thinking about having it done."

Teacher: "Have you considered all your options?"

Mary: "I don't see any other option available to me. I can't afford a baby, and my boyfriend and parents won't help."

Teacher: "There are people who do care and are willing to help you, including me."

Mary: "How could you help?"

Teacher: "Would you mind if we first take a moment to pray and ask God to help us know what He would like us to do?"

Mary: "No, I don't mind."

Teacher: "Dear heavenly Father, I know how much You love Mary and how much You love her baby. We are not sure what You want us to do, so we ask for Your wisdom and help. In Jesus' name, amen."

Mary: "What do you think I should do?"

Teacher: "Are you open to talking about possible options, besides abortion?"

Mary: "Yes, I'm open to hearing about them, but that doesn't mean I'll change my mind."

Teacher: "Have you considered adoption? Would you be willing to talk with someone who is a certified adoption specialist?"

Mary: "I haven't thought about adoption because I don't know how I could pay the expenses to even have the baby delivered."

Teacher: "If money was not a concern, would you be willing to keep the baby?"

Mary: "I would consider it, but I know nothing about being a parent. I'm only sixteen."

Teacher: "I know of several centers and clinics that have people who come alongside and minister to women who experience unplanned pregnancies. Oftentimes, these are young girls like yourself who are considering abortion. The staff and volunteers at these organizations love those girls regardless of the choices they make. If they choose to keep the baby, the staff and volunteers assist with financial support and classes on caring for a newborn baby, and managing a budget."

Mary: "I didn't know that, but it all sounds interesting. I would like to learn more about them."

Teacher: "If you give me some days and times that you would be available, I could arrange for a volunteer at one of the centers to meet with you and me."

Mary: "You would do that for me?"

Teacher: "Absolutely, I would be honored to do that for you. And if you decide to keep your baby, you can count on me to be your friend and walk through this with you."

Mary: "Why would you do that?"

Teacher: "Because the love of Jesus compels me to love you just as He has loved me. Do you know that Jesus loves you very much?"

Mary: "But what if I choose to have an abortion instead?"

Teacher: "Mary, although I hope and pray you will not choose to have an abortion and experience its serious consequences, I want you to know that if you do, I will still be your friend, and I will still love you. If you ever want to talk some more or pray together, come and see me. I will look forward to hearing from you regarding dates and times for us to visit my friends at the center."

In the first conversation, you can sense the Christian wants the girl to know the difference between right and wrong on the issue of abortion, as clearly as she sees it. But do you think Mary got the impression that the Christian truly cared about her as a person who is struggling? Though the teacher may have spoken words of truth, were they spoken in love? Did she communicate words of grace to a girl in need of compassion?

In the second conversation, a calm and peaceful tone exists that conveys sincere empathy for Mary. The Christian communicates in a way that says, "What you are thinking, feeling, and believing matters to me. You matter to me, regardless of whether your thinking is right or wrong." By asking questions and listening closely to Mary's answers, the teacher demonstrates other-minded respect for Mary. She doesn't tell her what to do, nor does she speak condescendingly in any way.

During the dialogue, do you think Mary felt loved, accepted and affirmed by the teacher? Did the words of the Christian communicate compassion, tenderness, and genuine concern for Mary? Did the teacher's responses indicate any desire to be "right," or was her motive to simply do what was right for this young girl? During the entire conversation, did the Christian ever compromise truth in any way?

With a humble servant's heart, the Christian makes herself available to be Mary's friend, reassuring her that she is not alone. As the Christian speaks the truth in love, and points Mary to God through prayer, she provides opportunity for Mary to experience the love of Christ.

Jesus said to him, I am the way, and the truth, and the life…
And you will know the truth, and the truth will set you free.

– John 14:6; 8:32 ESV

Instead, speaking the truth in love, we will in all things grow up into him who is the Head, that is, Christ.

– Ephesians 4:15

DISCUSSION QUESTIONS
CHAPTER 4

Seek and Speak the Truth in Love

1. Who did you most identify with in the conversations; the pregnant girl, or the teacher in the first conversation; the pregnant girl, or the teacher in the second conversation? Why?

2. In the first conversation, what was most important to the teacher? The girl? What was most important to each of them in the second conversation?

3. Page 42 encourages us to shift our focus from the issue to the relationship.

   a. *How does focusing on the relationship instead of the issue help us speak the truth in love?*

   b. *Which of the teacher's statements convey a focus on the relationship with Mary, the pregnant teen?*

   c. *Which statements convey truth spoken with grace and compassion?*

4. Prior to engaging in dialogue, why is it important to pray and identify what your focus and motive will be for wanting to talk with someone?

5. Read Galatians 6:1 and 2 Timothy 4:2. What do these verses tell us about how we can and should speak the truth in love?

6. In your group discussion this week, choose a current event in the news. For practice in Christlike dialogue, have two people practice engaging in conversation about the current event, while others in the group critique the dialogue.

GUIDELINE FOCUS: **JUDGE NOT**

REFRAIN FROM BEING CRITICAL OR JUDGEMENTAL OF OTHERS.

Look up Matthew 7:1-5, the verse on which this guideline is based, and copy it into your Journal in Appendix B on page 137. Also read and reflect upon Romans 2:1.

APPLICATION

In Chapter Two we were encouraged to **"Seize the Opportunity"**. Consider which topic or issue concerns you the most (i.e. concern for a family member or friend who does not yet know Jesus as their Savior and Lord, parent/child or family tensions, racial injustice, poverty, abortion, gender issues, conflict with employer or employee, differing generational perspectives, false teaching in churches, conflicting views on religion or politics, etc.).

On page 137 of the Journal in Appendix B, note one of these issues. Write out a prayer asking God to reveal to you ways that you can express His love and concern for anyone you know currently connected to that issue. Perhaps you can meet a physical need such as providing a meal or service. Perhaps you need to humbly ask for help from someone else who may have an area of expertise, like help with a home repair from a neighbor who is not a believer. **Seize the opportunities** to connect and relate in tangible, practical ways. Sometimes **"speaking" the truth** in love begins with acts of kindness and getting to truly know someone else.

Begin praying for confirmation that this person or group is someone God wants you to connect with and perhaps dialogue with. Prepare your heart to **seize the opportunity** to initiate dialogue and **speak the truth in love** to that person*. Remember two things: first, the mercy, kindness, and patience God has extended to you; and second, that without the Holy Spirit a person cannot discern spiritual truths (see 1 Corinthians 2:14).

*Make it clear to the person that your intention is for each of you to have an opportunity to share what you believe and why you believe as you do about the topic or issue of concern. Use this time to really listen to better understand what the other person believes and why they believe as they do.

PLAN AHEAD: *Next week's homework takes a bit more time. In addition to reading chapter five and completing the questions, plan ahead to schedule at least an hour in a quiet spot for some time to read and reflect on God's word.*

CHAPTER 5

GRACE, TRUTH, AND TOLERANCE

For the law was given through Moses; grace and truth came through Jesus Christ.

– John 1:17

Truth without grace breeds a self-righteous legalism that poisons the church and pushes the world away from Christ.

Grace without truth breeds moral indifference and keeps people from seeing their need for Christ.

When we offend everybody, it's because we've taken on the truth mantle without grace. When we offend nobody, it's because we've watered down truth in the name of grace.

If we minimize grace, the world sees no hope for salvation. If we minimize truth, the world sees no need for salvation. To show the world Jesus, we must offer unabridged grace and truth, emphasizing both, apologizing for neither.

People thirst for the real Jesus. Nothing less can satisfy.

We show people Jesus only when we show them grace and truth.

—Randy Alcorn, *The Grace and Truth Paradox*, pp. 18, 20, 87, 92

LOVE INCLUDES GRACE AND TRUTH

If the truth we speak is to be spoken in love, it is key that we remember the grace we have received from God. Only through an abiding relationship with Jesus Christ will His kindness and compassion flow through us to others. In his book, *Abiding in Christ* (p. 122), Andrew Murray says it this way:

> *Abiding in Him, you receive from Him His Spirit of love and compassion toward sinners, which makes you want to see them blessed. ...Abiding in Jesus, you come into contact with His infinite love, and its fire begins to burn within your heart; you see the beauty of love; you learn to look upon loving, serving, and saving your fellowmen as the highest privilege a disciple of Jesus can have.*

While some people may need to experience God's grace, mercy, and compassion, others may need loving truth and accountability. So, how does God want us to communicate that truth?

2 Timothy 4:2 teaches us to *correct, rebuke, and encourage – with great patience and careful instruction*. And in Galatians 6:1 we are reminded that loving discipline is to be administered *gently with humility*, not forgetting that we too are sinners saved by God's grace.

How can we know if the person we are discussing differences with is in need of grace, or in need of truth, or if that person is in need of both grace and truth? I know of only one certain way: **abide in Christ**. As we do, the Holy Spirit can help us discern the need and respond accordingly.

STAYING CLOSE TO THE VINE

In order to understand what it means to abide in Christ, allow these words from Jesus to really sink in:

"I am the vine; you are the branches. If a man remains in me and I in him, he will bear much fruit; apart from me you can do nothing" (John 15:5).

The word "abide" means to "remain in" and "act in accordance with". To abide or remain in Christ means to act in accordance with His will. Using the following analogy, we can learn what is required to maintain this abiding relationship with Jesus.

Consider the grapevine. The purpose for a grapevine's branches is to produce grapes, but without the branches being attached to the grapevine the grape production would be impossible. The branches receive food from the vine and when healthy, bear the vine's likeness.

A grapevine is pruned so that the branches remain close to the vine. Those branches that "remain" closest to the vine produce the healthiest grapes. But when the branches are not pruned, they begin to stray from the vine. The further they stray, the smaller they become, the less they produce, and the less they resemble their life giving vine.

It's not difficult to see what Jesus is getting at here. Christians (the branches, abiding in Christ, the Vine) are transformed into His own likeness. As we abide in Christ and stay close to Him, His Holy Spirit empowers and flows from us to produce spiritual fruit:

"But the fruit of the Spirit is love, joy, peace, patience, kindness, goodness, faithfulness, gentleness and self-control" (Galatians 5:22-23a).

Just as the healthiest grapes are those that remain closest to the grapevine, the Christians who are most like Jesus are those who remain closest to Him. This is a lifelong process that occurs day by day, and moment by moment as we take time to pray, study His Word, and faithfully trust and obey Him. The closer we remain to Jesus, the Vine, the more like Him we become. His interests become our interests. We value what He values. We become one in heart and mind with Him. In **1 John 2:24**, the apostle John wrote:

"See that what you have heard from the beginning remains in you. If it does, you also will remain in the Son and in the Father."

However, the Vine/branch analogy doesn't end there. John goes on to clarify in **1 John 3:11**:

"This is the message you heard from the beginning: We should love one another."

Jesus (the Vine) loves people. He desires His followers (the branches of the Vine), to experience Christlike love for others flowing through us as we engage in Christlike dialogue. If we abide in Christ, remaining in close fellowship with Jesus, His love will continue to flow through us. But if we stray from the Vine, our love for others will diminish over time. Therefore, the more we abide in Christ, the more effective our lives and conversations will be in bearing fruit for God's glory.

THE CLOSER WE REMAIN **to Jesus, the Vine,** THE MORE LIKE HIM WE BECOME.

AVOIDING FALSE GRACE AND HARSH TRUTH

Apart from Jesus Christ, most of us are at risk of erring in one of two ways: harsh truth, or false grace.

- **Harsh truth** is usually spoken when the motive is to enforce compliance.
- **False grace** occurs when we deceive ourselves into believing that being silent or showing sympathy is the most loving action we can take. But that simply isn't true in situations where the opposing party is in need of loving rebuke or admonishment.

We represent Jesus poorly when we communicate by way of either false grace or harsh truth. Harsh truth pushes people away from Christ. False grace fails to hold people accountable for actions or behavior that can hurt them physically or emotionally, hinder their fellowship with God, and keep them from maturing in Christ. Much like parents deal with their children, *The Lord disciplines those He loves* (Hebrews 12:6) and so we should hold fellow Christians accountable to do what is right, but we must remember to do so *gently, with humility, great patience,* and *careful instruction.*

When it comes to conflicts with unbelievers, the same principles apply, but it is important for Christians to remember 1 Corinthians 2:14. In all situations, we must ask God for His wisdom as He knows hearts, and we do not.

IS TOLERANCE LOVING?

Is tolerance an act of love? Or does it rather convey apathy, indifference and irresponsibility by failing to warn and discourage people from participating in behavior that can hurt them and others? It most likely depends on how one defines tolerance.

The world's definition of tolerance and the biblical definition of tolerance are quite different. The tolerance message of our world today not only teaches people to tolerate both sin and sinner, but to also condone the sinful practices and behaviors of others, even if those behaviors are displeasing to God, harmful to those who practice them, and detrimental to society. Christians must not be deceived into believing this lie, for to accept that lie would be to reject the absolute truth of the Word of God. Doing so would demonstrate a lack of love for the people who will be hurt, some eternally. Christians are called to care and be courageous enough to *speak the truth in love*, even to people ignorant of what the Word of God teaches. Always, however, we must speak as His humble, loving and gentle representatives.

As for God, He not only tolerates sinners (Romans 2:4), He loves them. While Jesus was here on earth, He engaged in conversation with all kinds of people from prostitutes, thieves and tax collectors to military leaders and religious rulers. In fact, the reason Jesus came to earth was to suffer and die to save sinners, because of His great love for us. But He never implied that sinful behavior was acceptable. As Jesus spoke with the woman caught in the act of adultery, He didn't condemn the woman, but He did tell her to leave her life of sin (John 8:11). As Christians, we are to follow Christ's example of loving sinners, yet never condoning sin.

While God loves sinners like you and me, He hates the wickedness and evil of sin. God's will for His people is for us to hate sin as He does:

"Your eyes are too pure to look on evil; you cannot tolerate wrong" (Habakkuk 1:13a).

"Love must be sincere. Hate what is evil; cling to what is good" (Romans 12:9).

In these next two conversations, the hope is for people to learn how to communicate in ways that convey love for a person without condoning something that God does not condone. As in other examples used in this study guide, the first conversation provides insight on how **not** to do it.

FIRST CONVERSATION: A CONSERVATIVE CHRISTIAN AND A GAY CHRISTIAN CO-WORKER

Two Christians, one gay and the other a heterosexual, have known each other for several years as employees in the same office. One day over lunch, they have a disagreement over homosexuality.

Conservative Christian: "Hey I saw you at my church on Sunday; I hadn't seen you there before."

Gay Christian: "Well, I thought I'd check it out. I've been reluctant to attend any church, as I'm gay. What do you think about gay relationships?"

Conservative Christian: "I really don't think they're okay. I think God hates homosexuality, sees it as sin, and views it as unnatural."

Gay Christian: "But, why? God made me that way. God doesn't make mistakes.

Conservative Christian: "I believe it's true that God doesn't make mistakes, but I don't believe God made you gay. Just look at it from an anatomical perspective. It's obvious that the genital parts of human beings were uniquely designed by God to work together naturally in a sexual relationship between a man and a woman. As a result of that relationship, women naturally have children. Have you ever heard of any natural birth of a child occurring as the result of a sexual encounter between two lesbians?"

Gay Christian: "Is love between two people only about sex? It's true, we can't have children naturally, but that doesn't mean we should be kept from adopting children and it doesn't mean we can't be good parents who love their children."

Conservative Christian: "I don't think that's right, as children need both a father and a mother."

Gay Christian: "So you dislike gay people because you don't think it's right, and because they don't see things exactly as you do. Is that correct?"

Conservative Christian: "I didn't say I didn't like gay people. I'm saying I think homosexuality is wrong."

Gay Christian: "Well, if you think homosexuality is sin, and wrong, and unnatural, then I would assume you don't think too highly of gay people either."

Conservative Christian: "I don't think too highly of homosexuality."

Gay Christian: "Then you don't think too highly of me, nor do most Christians, and that's why gay people don't feel loved and accepted by the majority of people who refer to themselves as Christians. The gay community views Christians as being judgmental and hypocritical when you are intolerant of people who don't see things exactly as you do. If you really loved people like the Bible teaches us to do, you would love all people, and you would give all people the freedom to choose what they think is best and right for them. I'm sorry I attended your church, but I won't make that mistake again."

Give thought as to how this conversation is an example of representing Jesus poorly.

SECOND CONVERSATION: A CONSERVATIVE CHRISTIAN AND GAY CHRISTIAN CO-WORKER

This is a Christlike dialogue as the two Christians engage in honest conversation. By asking questions and listening closely, the conservative Christian extends grace that affirms the person without compromising truth. There is an interest in the person and a desire to try and understand why this co-worker has chosen a gay lifestyle.

Conservative Christian: "Hey I saw you at my church on Sunday; I hadn't seen you there before."

Gay Christian: "Well, I thought I'd check it out. I've been reluctant to attend any church, as I'm gay. What do you think about gay relationships?"

Conservative Christian: "I'm glad you did, and I hope to see you there again. Before answering your question, let me ask you a question. How did it go at church yesterday? I hope you felt welcomed. I found that church after my divorce. The teaching I received at this church has really drawn me closer to Christ. I grew up in a Christian home believing that because I was a Christian I was a 'good person' and when I went through divorce I really felt like a bad person. The pastor helped me see that God came for broken people and we're all broken in some way. I learned a lot about 'truth' as a kid but it wasn't until recently that I have learned more about 'grace' and God is a God of truth and grace; you can't have one without the other. So how did it go for you?"

Gay Christian: "It was okay. I'd like to find a place where I can worship God and not be stared at. I went alone because Joe, my partner was out of town. Church people are usually pretty judgmental, hypocritical, and intolerant of gay people, so much for 'being known by our love for one another'. They don't like gay people, but part of me misses worshipping God with other believers. I heard your church was pretty welcoming and I saw lots of different kinds of people there so that was cool, but I'm pretty sure that if I showed up with Joe, it would be a different story."

Conservative Christian: "It makes me sad when I hear of Christians who have pushed people away from Christ by being judgmental and hypocritical, but do you think it is right to stereotype all Christians that way? Hey, I'm a Christian, and I haven't rejected you."

Gay Christian: "While I probably shouldn't stereotype *all* Christians that way, I'm just saying; it's been my experience that most are judgmental and critical of gay people."

Conservative Christian: "Do you have love for the Christians who you perceive to be falling short of representing Jesus well? Do you pray for them?"

Gay Christian: "No, I can't say I have much love for them, nor have I been praying for them."

Conservative Christian: "As you too are a Christian, don't you become just like you've described them to be, any time you withdraw your love for them and choose not to pray for them?"

Gay Christian: "Maybe so. I didn't think about that."

Conservative Christian: "What negative experiences have you personally encountered with a Christian or Christians over the issue of homosexuality?"

Gay Christian: "Avoidance. When Christians I've known heard I was gay, they have wanted nothing do with me."

Conservative Christian: "That's sad to hear, but hey, I'm a Christian and I'm still your friend."

Gay Christian: "I'm glad, but you don't approve of homosexuality either, do you?"

Conservative Christian: "I do not, and the reason I don't is because I do not believe a Christian should condone any behavior that God does not condone. That includes heterosexual Christians in sexual relationships outside of marriage, pornography, and any other sexually immoral behavior. In the Bible, sexual relations with someone of the same sex are mentioned in very negative ways, and also described as behavior that is unnatural. But instead of quoting those Scriptures that you likely already know, I'd like to hear your story, to try and understand where you are coming from."

Gay Christian: "Thank you, it's rare that someone ever asks to simply hear my story. I've been surrounded by Christians and Christianity my whole life. If the "church doors were open", our family was usually there. I remember going up to the altar to receive Jesus one night after a worship service—I was 8 years old then. I had this moment where I knew Jesus and His promises were real. But other difficult things were going on at that age. I felt different from the other boys. I wasn't a rough and tumble kid, but more artsy and more emotional. I began being bullied as early as 6 and 7. By the time I had asked Jesus into my life, the other boys were labeling me with words like "sissy" and even more harsh words. I mostly hung out with the girls.

By the time I reached puberty I began to realize my attractions towards the same gender. All my worst fears had come true. What would my parents think? Would I be rejected? How would Christians at church react? I always heard condemning messages about being gay in sermons. The Christian men at my church would make gay jokes. For a very long time I tried to repress all those feelings and prayed every night that God would take the attractions away. I even tried dating a few girls in high school but really only saw them as friends. I slowly got worn down. I stumbled on some pornography around that same time and then found gay pornography and it became an addiction.

Eventually in college, I began exploring some of the "gay affirming" Christian organizations on campus. I had finally found a place where I felt like I could be me—no more lying, no more repressing. I finally came out to my parents. They were very hurt and angry. We still have rocky conversations that just leave me feeling shame and a failure. I continue to look for a church that will accept me as a gay man. That's why I was checking out your church."

Conservative Christian: "First of all, I want to personally apologize and to apologize on behalf of any Christians who have been critical and judgmental of gay people without ever taking the time to get to know someone and listen to their story.

Have you wrestled with your faith on this journey? I'd like to hear how you interpret Scripture, as it relates to what you believe the Bible says in regard to husbands and wives in contrast to the gay lifestyle."

Gay Christian: "Yeah, you can see that I've been in conflict with my faith and sexuality for a long time. It's been a very painful and difficult process. Now that I've come out and am admitting that I am a gay Christian, I don't feel so conflicted anymore and I feel better about myself.

I have read and reread all the scriptures on homosexuality over and over all these years. It always made me fearful that God hated me. The campus ministry I mentioned earlier helped me to understand these scriptures in a new light. A lot of the Old and New Testament passages don't seem to mention a loving monogamous gay relationship. The homosexuality referenced seems to be more equated to violence, abuse and male prostitution. Jesus never even mentions homosexuality at all. He preaches love and fidelity—the very thing that I want from a marriage partner."

Conservative Christian: "Jesus does teach of love and fidelity within a marriage between a male and female. In Ephesians 5:22-33, the love relationship between a husband and wife in marriage is a way of visualizing the gospel; man and woman - Christ and His bride, the church - like and unlike, come together in an intimate love relationship. In Matthew 19 when Jesus is asked about divorce, He goes back to Genesis 1 to remind us that God made us male and female. It is because we are male and female that we have this thing called marriage where a man shall leave his father and mother and be united to his wife, and the two shall become one flesh. Within this definition of marriage how do you view gay couples? How do you believe God views gay couples?"

Gay Christian: "Not sure. I haven't considered that. What about the reality that fifty percent of Christian marriages end in divorce? I guess my concern is, can you be affirming of gays?"

Conservative Christian: "First, I do not condone divorce as God does not condone divorce. Yet I still love people who are divorced. I hope other Christians feel the same way, as I'm divorced. Second, I can affirm that a gay man or a lesbian may care as much for their partner as a husband cares for his wife, or a wife for her husband. Yet I do not condone homosexuality because I affirm God's intent for marriage to be between a man and woman, with sexual relations to occur only between a husband and his wife."

Gay Christian: "If you believe that to be true and you think homosexuality is sin, how can you remain my friend?"

Conservative Christian: "If Christians withdrew our love and friendship from people who sin, none of us would have any friends. Pre-marital sex is sin, extra-marital sex is sin. Jesus even said that *anyone who looks at a woman lustfully has already committed adultery with her in his heart (Matthew 5:28)*. We all stand in need of God's grace, so I have no problem in being your friend, and there are many other heterosexual Christians who have love for friends who are gay or lesbian, but my question to you is this, "Will you withdraw your friendship from me because I choose to not condone something I believe God clearly does not condone?"

Gay Christian: "To be honest, it's hard to hear your perspective. And we seem to be at a place of "agreeing to disagree" with one another. But what's true is it's not fair for me to ask you to give up your convictions—any more than it is for you to ask for me to give up mine. Hopefully we can work on building trust in our friendship and continue to dialogue."

Give thought as to how this conversation is an example of representing Jesus well. For more information on this topic, consider reading Sam Allbery's book, *Is God anti-gay and other questions about homosexuality.*

AVOID CONFORMITY TO THIS WORLD

In his letter to Roman Christians Paul warned them, *Do not conform any longer to the pattern of this world, but be transformed by the renewing of your mind* (Romans 12:2a). We as Christians of today will be wise to heed Paul's admonishment, for there are many ways in which Christians have ignored the spiritual, and conformed to what is worldly.

Embracing the world's definition of tolerance is one such example. Forsaking what the Bible teaches about hating evil, many Christians have allowed the world to deceive them into believing that it is unloving and judgmental of anyone who is not accepting of the sinful behavior of others, even though it is unacceptable to God and harmful to society. If we complacently embrace that lie, we become worldly, rather than influencing the world for Christ. Christians should not be deceived into tolerating and condoning any willful sinful behavior that God does not condone.

Christians also conform to this world when we are unloving toward people with whom we experience conflict. If two Christians are unwilling to maintain their love for one another while discussing their differences, how is that any different from how any average person would respond? What if the disagreement is with a person who is not a Christian?

Will the Christian be mindful of the fact that the non-Christian hasn't yet come to a saving knowledge of the truth, and doesn't understand how much their sinful behavior grieves their loving Creator?

If the Christian responds with truth, but without kindness and compassion, that Christian has *forgotten that he has been cleansed from his past sins* (2 Peter 1:3-9), and has failed to *remember the kindness and mercy* God has extended to him (Titus 3:3-7).

MEETING NEEDS

If we are to represent Jesus well by way of Christlike dialogue, meeting the needs of the person we are talking with should be given high priority during our conversation. As we are referring to communication and dialogue, the focus is on meeting emotional and spiritual needs, rather than physical needs.

Three **emotional needs** of people are:

- To be loved
- To be accepted
- To be affirmed

Two primary **spiritual needs** are:

- For people to know Jesus Christ as their Lord and Savior – Salvation
- For Christians to mature in Christ as we trust and obey Jesus as Lord – Sanctification

So how do we extend grace without compromising truth? How does one communicate absolute truth in love to those who believe in relativism? How do we convey godly tolerance toward sinners, without condoning worldly tolerance of sin? And how can we know if someone with an opposing view is in need of grace and mercy, truth and accountability, or some of each?

There's only one certain way: **abide in Christ**. Why? Because Christ knows every person's heart, and we don't. But if we abide in Christ, remain focused on His interests and His will, we can through the power of His Holy Spirit discern a person's need and convey grace and truth in ways that meet needs for God's glory.

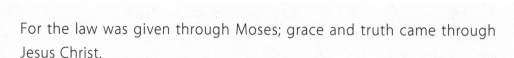

For the law was given through Moses; grace and truth came through Jesus Christ.

– John 1:17

DISCUSSION QUESTIONS
CHAPTER 5

Grace, Truth, and Tolerance

1. Two of Jesus' life-changing dialogues help us learn how to meet the emotional and spiritual needs of people by extending grace and speaking truth.

   a. *Read John 3:1-21. What was the common ground and how did Jesus use truth to meet the spiritual need of Nicodemus?*

   b. *Read John 4:1-26. What was the common ground and how did Jesus use grace to meet the emotional needs of the Samaritan woman, and truth to meet her spiritual need?*

c. *What have you learned from Jesus' conversations with Nicodemus and the woman at the well that you can put into practice as you engage in conversations with people of opposing views?*

2. In which way are you more prone to err, on the side of false grace, or harsh truth? Discuss the possible consequences of responding in each of these two ways. Share personal experiences.

3. Read Mark 11:15-18.

a. *What can we learn about tolerance from Jesus' forceful response to the money changers?*

b. *Is it okay for followers of Jesus to respond to people in similar ways? Why or why not? Justify your answer with Scripture.*

c. *What amazed the crowd hearing Jesus' words and observing His actions (See v. 18), and what can we learn from Jesus' response to the money changers that can prepare us for engaging in conversations that honor God?*

4. Read Leviticus 20:13 and Romans 1:24-27. What does the Bible say about homosexuality, and what are possible negative consequences that are likely to occur when Christians start believing the world's definition of tolerance, and begin to condone sin of any kind?

GUIDELINE FOCUS: **BE TEACHABLE**

REMAIN OPEN TO THE POSSIBILITY OF BEING WRONG ABOUT YOUR POSITION, AND TO THE POSSIBILITY OF BEING DECEIVED.

Look up Proverbs 3:5-6, Jeremiah 17:9, and James 1:26, the verses on which this guideline is based and copy one or two of them into your Journal in Appendix B on page 138.

APPLICATION

This week spend an hour in quiet reflection. Abiding in Christ and being taught by Him begins with reflecting on God's word. Only during fellowship with Him, can we truly come to know God intimately and be taught by Him. As you abide in Christ ask Him what He may want to teach you about yourself, your beliefs, and the words and ways you speak to others. Here are some ideas to get you started:

- Read John 15: 1-12.

- Copy your memory verses onto the space provided in the Journal on page 138 and note the key points God is teaching you.

- Review both the Application Sections for your Journal entries for the first four chapters (pages 131-137). Use these responses to discern what changes or action steps God desires you to take.

- Is there someone God brings to mind as you pray? Is there a broken relationship, a relationship that has grown cold, or a person or people group you have stereotyped, gossiped about and/or withdrawn your love from?

- As you pray, journal anything God reveals to you from His word and this quiet time.

If God is prompting you to initiate a Christlike dialogue with someone, remember:

- to pray for the Holy Spirit to join the conversation and grant you God's help to discern emotional and spiritual needs and show you how He wants to use what you have learned so far to meet those needs.

- the great kindness, patience, mercy and grace of God that led you to repentance.

- people are at different stages of spiritual maturity. Non-Christians do not have the Holy Spirit so they cannot understand the things that come from the Spirit of God (See 1 Corinthians 2:14).

- to listen well.

CHAPTER 6

FOCUS ON CHRIST'S INTERESTS

For everyone looks out for their own interests, not those of Jesus Christ.

– Philippians 2:21

There can only be two basic loves, the love of God unto the forgetfulness of self, or the love of self unto the forgetfulness of God.

—Augustine

FOCUS ON CHRIST'S INTERESTS

If we are to engage in Christlike dialogue, we need an ongoing awareness of Christ's two primary interests:

1. Salvation – for people to believe in and receive Jesus as their Savior and Lord.

    "Here is a trustworthy saying that deserves full acceptance: "Christ Jesus came into the world to save sinners… " (1 Timothy 1:15).

2. Sanctification – for Christians to *obey* Jesus as Lord and become more like Him.

    "Until we all reach unity in the faith and in the knowledge of the Son of God and become mature, attaining to the whole measure of the fullness of Christ" (Ephesians 4:13).

INCLUDE JESUS IN THE CONVERSATION

A pastor was aware of a New Age bookstore in his community that had a coffee shop inside. He saw it as a great opportunity to get acquainted with people who had not yet come to know Jesus.

One day, as he was about to leave the bookstore, he approached the checkout counter and asked the clerk, "What is your opinion of Christians?"

As the clerk observed the pastor's Bible, his response to the question was, "Oh, they're okay; they're fine."

Convinced he hadn't heard the truth, the pastor pushed his Bible aside, looked the clerk in the eyes, and asked, "Now, what do you really think of Christians?"

This time the clerk gave his honest answer: "I think they are arrogant, critical, judgmental, and they treat me like I'm a bad person."

The pastor replied, "Jesus isn't like that." He then began to share with the clerk how Jesus treated the Samaritan woman at the well, and the woman caught in adultery. The pastor explained that Jesus didn't turn them away because they were sinners. Instead, He loved them by extending grace and compassion, while never condoning their sin.

Excited by this new revelation, the clerk told the pastor that the owner of the bookstore, who was also a city councilman, needed to hear that message. Later that day, the clerk gave the pastor's telephone number to his boss.

Early the next morning, the owner of the bookstore called the pastor and asked if he would meet him for breakfast at 7:30 a.m. The pastor rearranged his schedule to meet with the owner.

For quite some time, the pastor listened attentively while the owner shared his negative views of Christians. When the man finished talking, the pastor replied, "Jesus isn't like that." He went on to share what Jesus is like, according to what the Bible says.

After their dialogue, the pastor invited the man to a Sunday service at his church and asked if he would share with the entire congregation his thoughts on how people claiming to be Christians are perceived by people who are not Christians. The man accepted the invitation, and on that Sunday he addressed the entire congregation. When he finished sharing, the pastor laid his arm around the man's shoulder and prayed for him. With tears in his eyes, the councilman looked out at the congregation and said, "If all of you would treat people in this city the way your pastor has treated me, you could turn this city around."

REPRESENTING JESUS WELL

How did the pastor treat the man? Without ever saying so, the pastor showed the man that all Christians are not as the councilman perceived them to be. He modeled **Christlikeness** in the following ways:

- **He communicated grace by asking questions and listening in order to meet the man's emotional need for love, acceptance, and affirmation.**

- **He communicated truth to meet his spiritual need to know Jesus by saying, "Jesus isn't like that" and using the Word of God to explain and affirm what Jesus is like.**

Just think of the impact God's people can have for Christ if we begin to embrace disagreements and controversial issues as opportunities to put Christlike dialogue into practice. As we humbly listen to people, and then speak the truth in love, we communicate in ways that draw people to Jesus, rather than push them away.

ASK GOOD QUESTIONS; LISTEN CLOSELY

Evangelist and author, Garry Poole modeled a great example of how to focus on Christ's interests in conversation with people who don't see things exactly as we do. Garry invited five people who were not yet Christians to participate in a panel discussion at the weekend church services where he would be the interviewer and moderator. They accepted his invitation and shared openly before the entire congregation. After asking a question, Garry listened closely as each person gave their answer. Because Garry listened closely to hear each panel member's response, they felt heard, appreciated, and respected, but Garry didn't stop there. During the interview, Garry also shared a passage of Scripture with each question. Panel members knew in advance that this would be the process so there were no surprises, and the ones that chose to be interviewed were open to hearing what the Bible said on each of the topics that were discussed. By bringing Christ into the conversation through Scripture, the dialogue became not just an exercise in good listening, but a Christlike dialogue. Here are some of the questions Garry asked, a few of the panel's responses, and Scripture to consider with the question:

Question: "What do you believe about the Bible?"

Response: "It is man written, not direct Word of God."

Scripture: "All Scripture is God-breathed and is useful for teaching, rebuking, correcting and training in righteousness" (2 Timothy 3:16).

"Above all, you must understand that no prophecy of Scripture came about by the prophet's own interpretation. For prophecy never had its origin in the will of man, but men spoke from God as they were carried along by the Holy Spirit" (2 Peter 1:20-21).

Question: "Who is Jesus?"

Response: "A great teacher, but not deity. I don't believe Jesus died on the cross, but if He did, that's a real game-changer."

Scripture: "When Jesus came to the region of Caesarea Philippi, he asked his disciples... "Who do you say I am?" Simon Peter answered, "You are the Christ, the Son of the living God." Jesus replied, "Blessed are you, Simon son of Jonah, for this was not revealed to you by man, but by my Father in heaven" (Matthew 16:13, 15-17).

The angel said to the women, "Do not be afraid, for I know that you are looking for Jesus, who was crucified. He is not here; he has risen, just as

he said. Come and see the place where he lay. Then go quickly and tell his disciples: 'He has risen from the dead, and is going ahead of you into Galilee. There you will see him.' Now I have told you" (Matthew 28:5-7).

Question: "What happens after you die?"

Response: "I don't believe in heaven or hell."

Scripture: "Then they will go away to eternal punishment, but the righteous to eternal life" (Matthew 25:46).

"Multitudes who sleep in the dust of the earth will awake: some to everlasting life, others to shame and everlasting contempt" (Daniel 12:2).

As the interview and conversation concluded, the panel provided insightful answers to these final questions:

Question: "How confident are you in your answers?"

Response: "I am very unsure. There is no certainty to what I believe."

Scripture: "And this is the testimony: God has given us eternal life, and this life is in his Son. He who has the Son has life; he who does not have the Son of God does not have life. I write these things to you who believe in the name of the Son of God so that you may know that you have eternal life" (1 John 5:11-13).

Question: "On a scale of 1-10, with 10 being the most open, how open are you to having these kind of spiritual conversations?"

Response: "9-10 depending upon how we would be approached." One person added,

> *The majority of people want to talk about what they believe,*
> *but most Christians don't listen.*

Question: "What is your advice to Christians on how to engage in spiritual conversations with people who are not Christians?"

Response: "First listen to my story. Don't come for a debate about who is right or wrong. Don't come with a sermon. Come for conversation."

Scripture: **"My dear brothers, take note of this: Everyone should be quick to listen, slow to speak..." (James 1:19).**

This panel presentation in front of the entire congregation was an excellent example of an intentional focus on Christ's interests throughout the dialogue.

A concern for those who are in need of salvation was expressed by providing an opportunity for non-believers to share openly about what they believe. They felt heard. Truth was spoken in love as Scripture was shared in the conversation and genuine love and concern were expressed as some of us spent time with the panel throughout the weekend getting to know them and sharing meals with them.

The congregation was blessed to experience and learn from an example of evangelistic listening. Compassion for the lost was cultivated as the audience grew in deeper understanding of the Great Commission. Many were moved by the panels' responses and began to see people more clearly through the eyes of Jesus. It was a great opportunity for us to grow and mature in Christ as we were reminded of God's great love for people and His desire to see people come to know Him for who He truly is.

First listen to my story.
DON'T COME FOR A DEBATE
ABOUT WHO IS RIGHT OR WRONG.
Don't come with a sermon.
COME FOR CONVERSATION.

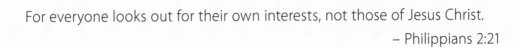

For everyone looks out for their own interests, not those of Jesus Christ.

– Philippians 2:21

DISCUSSION QUESTIONS
CHAPTER 6

Focus on Christ's Interests

1. What have you learned from this chapter that can help you represent Jesus well when engaging in spiritual conversations with people who do not yet know Jesus as their Savior?

2. List the names of the non-Christian acquaintances or friends you have and that you know and interact with regularly. Copy their names into your Journal in Appendix B on page 139. These could be people in your family, workplace, neighborhood… If you do not have any non-Christians in your circle of influence, what might you do to begin to interact regularly with non-Christians? Consider your hobbies and interests and where you live and work. What other ideas does your group have for engaging the lost in spiritual conversations?

3. Read 1 Thessalonians 5:23-24; Colossians 3:12-14; John 15:5, 8; Galatians 5:22-23. In what ways do these verses help prepare you to represent Jesus well through Christlike dialogue?

4. Read 2 Peter 1:5-9 and 1 John 4:20-21. From these passages of Scripture, what do you learn about Christ's interests and how knowing those interests prepare you to represent Jesus well when engaging in a Christlike dialogue with someone who doesn't see things exactly as you do?

GUIDELINE FOCUS: **PURSUE TRUTH**

AGREE TO GIVE ONE ANOTHER THE FREEDOM TO SPEAK THE TRUTH AS EACH PERCEIVES IT, WITHOUT INTERRUPTION FROM THE OTHER(S), EXCEPT TO ASK QUESTIONS FOR CLARIFICATION. AGREE TO CONSIDER THE BIBLE AS A RELIABLE SOURCE OF TRUTH AND WISDOM FOR LIFE'S CHALLENGES.

Look up, Psalm 51:6; John 14:6, 8:32, the verses on which this guideline is based and copy one of them into your Journal in Appendix B on page 139. Take some time this week to review and reflect on the verses you have written in your journal. Consider committing these verses to memory.

APPLICATION

Read 1 Peter 3:15. Pray over the list of people you identified in Question 2. Ask God to make you aware of one person who is not yet a Christian whom He would like you to intentionally connect with more deeply and perhaps have an opportunity to share the story of your own relationship with Christ. Your life story or "testimony" is an effective way of sharing the truth of the gospel and it is important to be prepared to share it with others. Complete the template provided on pages 146-147 in the Journal in Appendix C, and be prepared to practice telling your story in your group. Depending on the size of the group, it may be necessary for some of you to share this week and some to share after Chapter 7.

PLAN AHEAD: *In Chapter 7 you will invite this person to engage in dialogue and share your stories. Plan to arrange a time that would work for you to connect over coffee or dinner.*

CHAPTER 7

TRUST GOD WITH THE OUTCOME

When they hurled their insults at him, he did not retaliate; when he suffered, he made no threats. Instead, he entrusted himself to him who judges justly.

– 1 Peter 2:23

The Power of Lamb-Likeness

We may well ask what gives the Blood its power!

Not the Blood of the Warrior, but the Blood of the Lamb! In other words, that which gives the precious Blood its power with God for men is the lamb-like disposition of the One who shed it. ...But the title "the Lamb" has a deeper meaning. It describes His character. He is the Lamb in that He is meek and lowly in heart, gentle and unresisting, and all the time surrendering His own will to the Father's for the blessing and saving of men. Anyone but the Lamb would have resented and resisted the treatment men gave Him. But He, in obedience to the Father and out of love for us, did neither. Men did what they liked to Him and for our sakes He yielded all the time. When He was reviled, He reviled not again. When He suffered, He threatened not. No standing up for His rights, no hitting back, no resentment, no complaining! How different from us! ...the nailing and the lifting up, the piercing of His side and the flowing of His Blood—none of these things would ever have been, had He not been the Lamb. ...And all that to pay the price of my sin! So we see He is not merely the Lamb because He died on the Cross, but He died upon the Cross because He is the Lamb.

Let us ever see this disposition in the Blood…. Humility, lamb-likeness, the surrender of our wills to God, are what He looks for supremely from man.

—Roy Hession, Calvary Road, pp. 98-101

TRUST GOD WITH THE OUTCOME

If we truly employ the fourth characteristic of *Christlike Dialogue* and trust God with the outcome, the anxiety that normally accompanies conflict should disappear.

One day I was about to meet someone to discuss our differences. Before I did, I remember saying to a friend, "I wonder why I have so much anxiety about this. I just want to share my perspective."

To which my friend replied, "You probably want to control the outcome."

I said, "That's right. I do want to control the outcome."

What I learned from that conversation with my friend was that any time we have a strong desire to be "right", win the argument, get our way and control the outcome, we can expect to have anxiety. When we choose to trust God with the outcome, and wait patiently on Him to work in the hearts of people, including ours, we can experience peace in the midst of conflict.

For example, when we engage people with differing views, most people believe their view is the correct view. If you are a Christian and you are having a spiritual conversation about important matters, you think what the Bible says is true and you want others to agree. The problem with that thinking is that many people do not believe the Bible is true. If you want to argue with them about it, you will have a debate. But if you want to engage in a Christlike dialogue, plan to speak the truth in love and then trust God with the outcome. Don't demand or expect people to see things exactly as you do. It is ultimately the Holy Spirit who brings people to a knowledge and understanding of spiritual truth.

This is one of the lessons we can learn from the *Lamb of God*. He was right, but He did not demand that people agree with Him. That cost Jesus His life, but think of the lives that have been saved by His willingness to surrender to the will and ways of His Father.

WHAT IS YOUR SOURCE OF TRUTH?

Most people have their own point of view on any given topic that interests them. But how does one determine which of the many existing opinions is accurate and reliable? What is their foundational source that most influenced the beliefs they convey?

There are many perceived sources of truth, such as the media, television and movies, friends, family, Google, one's intellect, the Torah, the Quran, and the Bible to name a few.

When discussing important matters, it's important to identify one's source of truth applicable to the issue or topic, and to question the reliability of that source. We all have the freedom to choose what or who our sources are, but it doesn't mean we have to agree with the choice others make. The *Christlike Dialogue* guideline we mentioned in the last chapter, PURSUE TRUTH, directs us to consider the Bible as a reliable source of truth, which is the primary source of truth for any true Christian.

Kent, a good friend of mine, hosted a *Christlike Dialogue* seminar at his church. At the time, he was the executive director of a ministry for international students. After attending the seminar, Kent used the *Christlike Dialogue* guidelines for initiating Christlike dialogue between Muslims from nearby colleges and universities and a few Christians. He invited me to join them.

Prior to our first meeting, we agreed to choose a discussion topic that was of interest to everyone. We added that we were not looking for individuals' opinions in regard to the topic, but rather, we'd like participants to share what each one's source of truth said about the topic.

We initially agreed to meet once a month, but everyone enjoyed the dialogue so much we ended up meeting once a week for the entire summer. Each week we would choose a topic to discuss, such as heaven and hell or the roles of husband and wife. The Muslim students would share what the Quran, their source of truth, taught and the Christians would share what the Bible, our source of truth, said on the topic.

As we listened to each other, it gave us a better understanding of what we believe and why we believe as we do. Each person had the freedom to continue believing as they did, or to embrace a new perspective.

It was a real privilege and blessing to meet and engage in conversations with twelve young Muslims during that summer. Close friendships were built and some continue over a decade later.

I learned a lot from our time together, including how important it is for anyone engaging in Christlike dialogue with a person of another faith to discuss these questions:

- What is your understanding of who Jesus is?
- How does a person receive forgiveness of sins and eternal life with God?
- What happens after we die?
- What is your source of truth upon which you base your answers?
- Is your source of truth reliable? If yes, what do you base that on?

When we CHOOSE TO TRUST GOD WITH THE OUTCOME, **and wait patiently on Him to work in the hearts of people, including ours, we can** EXPERIENCE PEACE IN THE MIDST OF CONFLICT.

Christians and Muslims should show love and respect for each other as fellow human beings made in the image of God. While there is common ground that we can agree upon, there are also significant differences between the teachings of the Christian's source of truth, the Bible and the Muslim's source of truth, the Quran. We will explore some of each.

Christian: "Thank you for your willingness to discuss a few similarities and differences between the teachings of Islam and Christianity with me."

Muslim: "Thank you for initiating this dialogue. These conversations are important to expanding knowledge of religion, both our own and each other's, especially when grounded in mutual respect."

Christian: "As we proceed, let's remind each other to support our answers with words from our sources of truth, rather than just give our opinions. Is that okay with you?"

Muslim: "Certainly. The Quran is the main source of truth and legislation for Muslims, therefore it's considered the ultimate authority."

Christian: "What does it mean for the Quran to be the main source of legislation?"

Muslim: "It's the first and primary source Muslims go to when they need guidance and answers to many issues and questions in life. Of course scholars and Imams provide additional guidance with interpretation and advice but the starting point is always the Quran."

Christian: "Thank you for clarifying that. My prayer is for God to use our dialogue to help us learn from each other what we believe. I also pray that God would give us a greater understanding of Himself and of His truth. Is there anything you would like to add to that prayer?"

Muslim: "Amen! (This term is used in Islam as well!) Couldn't have said it better."

Christian: "Before discussing our differences, let's establish some common ground. What would you say the teachings of Islam and Christianity have in common, and what is a good reason for us to take time to dialogue?"

Muslim: "I'll begin with the basics. In order to be a Muslim, you must believe in Christianity, the Virgin Mary, and her son Jesus. In Islam, Jesus is believed to be a prophet and the Messiah (to return on Judgment Day). One of Islam's five pillars is the belief in God's books and prophets who preceded the prophet Mohammed (Abraham, Moses, etc.). For Muslims, Islam is the continuation of God's message to humans and as such a continuation of what Christianity and Jesus brought to humanity. The Virgin Mary is mentioned in the Quran 24 times. Jesus Christ is mentioned 25 times. The Quran teaches Muslims that they worship the same God as Christians. One God.

The best reason for a dialogue like this is to open people's minds to how similar the teachings are, that ultimately we all worship the same God who sent us the same message."

Christian: "The Bible proclaims the virgin birth of Jesus, that Mary is the mother of Jesus, that Jesus was a prophet and the Messiah who will return, and that there is one true God. But I question your statement that "ultimately we all worship the same God who sent us the same message" as the Quran and Bible have such contradictory messages regarding who Jesus is and how people are saved from our sins and reconciled to God, all of great significance in this life and in determining our eternal destiny. Before we take time to discuss our differences, what else would you say the teachings of the Quran and the Bible have in common? And please be sure to ask any questions you would like to ask during our conversation."

Muslim: "To focus on the similarities, we do believe the same messages are consistent among all faiths (as in 10 commandments), and much of the same teachings and stories of prophets in the Holy books (Torah, Gospel, & Quran). A few more examples are belief in the day of judgement, an afterlife, the existence of heaven and hell, and, of course, endless aspects emphasized for daily life like charity, forgiveness, truthfulness, and seeking knowledge."

Christian: "Thank you for sharing those. It's great to know we have a common interest in such things as charity, forgiveness, truthfulness, and seeking knowledge. I hope more Christians and Muslims will meet and talk about what their sources of truth say about each of the topics you mentioned. There's a great need for people of different religions to engage in conversations that honor God, instead of gossiping or stereotyping one another. Do you agree, and would you like to add anything to that statement?"

Muslim: "Absolutely. We are often misinformed and take stereotypes to be true without ever having conversed with someone from that religion. Sometimes we just don't have any knowledge of other religious beliefs and practices. I have even been surprised to learn of commonalities between Islam and Buddhism when a Korean-American friend shares from her religion! Differences are easy to point at, but the commonalities, that may take a little time to uncover, are invaluable."

Christian: "While it's important to consider what we have in common, exploring differences is crucial for the purpose of determining if the teachings of our sources of truth contradict and compromise the central doctrine of one another's faith in any way. So let's each share one or two primary differences between the teachings of the Quran versus the teachings of the Bible that concern us the most, okay? You go first."

Muslim: "The belief in Jesus being God himself and the son of God constitutes the primary difference to Muslims who believe in God's divinity and no one else. To Muslims, Jesus is a prophet of God, not his son. The Quran tells us the story of Mary's virginity and how she bore Jesus without a human touch, but this is considered a miracle of God. Both Mary and Jesus are considered as humans to Muslims. The other point of contention for Muslims is Christian's disbelief in Mohammed's message as a continuation of their own, particularly since Muslims believe in Jesus and Christianity."

"And remember when the angels said, "O Mary, God sends you the good news of a Command of His: his name shall be Messiah, Jesus son of Mary. He will be highly honored in this world and in the Next World and he will be among those favored by God." Quran 3:45

"Hearing this, Mary said, "How, O Lord, shall I have a son, when no man has ever touched me?" "Thus shall it be," was the answer. God creates whatever He wills. When He decrees a thing, He only says, "Be" and it is." Quran 3:47

Christian: "We learn from the Bible of the virgin birth, and that Mary bore Jesus without a human touch. It was a miracle of God. In the Bible, both Mary and Jesus are humans. The difference is that the Bible also declares the divinity of Jesus, making Him fully human and fully God. I agree that the primary difference between the teachings of the Quran and the Bible are in regard to who Jesus truly is. Here are a few verses from the Bible about the virgin birth, that Jesus is the Son of God, and that Jesus is God:

VIRGIN BIRTH

"In the sixth month of Elizabeth's pregnancy, God sent the angel Gabriel to Nazareth, a town in Galilee, to a virgin pledged to be married to a man named Joseph, a descendant of David. The virgin's name was Mary. The angel went to her and said, "Greetings, you who are highly favored! The Lord is with you." Mary was greatly troubled at his words and wondered what kind of greeting this might be. But the angel said to her, "Do not be afraid, Mary; you have found favor with God. You will conceive and give birth to a son, and you are to call him Jesus" (Luke 1:26-31).

JESUS IS THE SON OF GOD

"And when Jesus was baptized, immediately he went up from the water, and behold, the heavens were opened to him, and he saw the Spirit of God descending like a dove and coming to rest on him; and behold, a voice from heaven said, "This is my beloved Son, with whom I am well pleased" (Matthew 3:16-17).

"When Jesus came to the region of Caesarea Philippi, he asked his disciples,..."Who do you say I am?"

Simon Peter answered, "You are the Christ, the Son of the living God."

Jesus replied, "Blessed are you, Simon son of Jonah, for this was not revealed to you by man, but by my Father in heaven" (Matthew 16:13, 15-17).

JESUS IS GOD

"In the beginning was the Word, and the Word was with God, and the Word was God.

The Word became flesh and made his dwelling among us. We have seen his glory, the glory of the one and only Son, who came from the Father, full of grace and truth.

For the law was given through Moses; grace and truth came through Jesus Christ. No one has ever seen God, but the one and only Son, who is himself God and is in closest relationship with the Father, has made him known" (John 1:1, 14, 17-18).

Muslim: "No doubt this issue of the trinity is one of the main differences between some branches of Christianity and Islam. Muslims are taught, that just like all the prophets sent before him, Jesus, while holy and born of virgin birth, is also a man. The most well-known and recited verses on this are the following:

"People of the Book, do not go to excess in your religion, and do not say anything about God except the truth: the Messiah, Jesus, son of Mary, was nothing more than a messenger of God, His word, directed to Mary, a spirit from Him. So believe in God and His messengers and do not speak of a 'Trinity'—stop, that is better for you—God is only one God, He is far above having a son, everything in the heavens and earth belongs to Him and He is the best one to trust." Quran 4:171-173

"Say: He is God, the One and Only; God, the Eternal, Absolute; He begetteth not, nor is He begotten; And there is none like unto Him." Quran 112:1-4

Christian: "Here are additional verses from the Bible regarding God's only begotten Son, sources of truth, and the Trinity."

GOD'S ONLY BEGOTTEN SON

"For God so loved the world, that He gave His only begotten Son, that whoever believes in Him shall not perish, but have eternal life. For God did not send the Son into the world to judge the world, but that the world might be saved through Him. He who believes in Him is not judged; he who does not believe has been judged already, because he has not believed in the name of the only begotten Son of God" (John 3:16-18).

SOURCES OF TRUTH (Jesus, the Holy Spirit, the Bible)

Jesus answered, "I am the way and the truth and the life. No one comes to the Father except through me" (John 14:6).

[Jesus said,] "If you love me, keep my commands. And I will ask the Father, and he will give you another advocate to help you and be with you forever—the Spirit of truth.

   But when he, the Spirit of truth, comes, he will guide you into all the truth" (John 14:15-17a; 16:13a).

"Sanctify them in the truth; your word is truth" (John 17:17, ESV).

THE TRINITY (One God as Father, Son, and Holy Spirit acting in perfect unity with one another)

"Then Jesus came to them and said, 'All authority in heaven and on earth has been given to me. Therefore go and make disciples of all nations, baptizing them in the name of the Father and of the Son and of the Holy Spirit, and teaching them to obey everything I have commanded you. And surely I am with you always, to the very end of the age'" (Matthew 28:18-20).

"Earlier, you mentioned another point of contention for Muslims is, "Christian's disbelief in Mohammed's message as a continuation of their own, particularly since Muslims believe in Jesus and Christianity."

True Christianity and the Bible proclaim Jesus is the Son of God. Islam and the Quran teach Muslims to reject and deny this foundational truth. So I hope you understand why we disagree with your statement, "Muslims believe in Jesus and Christianity".

I have disbelief in any message that has altered the biblical text in any way, as there are stern warnings with serious consequences for adding anything or taking any words away from its words of prophecy, as confirmed by this quote from the Bible:

"I warn everyone who hears the words of the prophecy of this book: if anyone adds to them, God will add to him the plagues described in this book, and if anyone takes away from the words of the book of this prophecy, God will take away his share in the tree of life and in the holy city, which are described in this book" (Revelation 22:18-19).

Muslim: "Of course there are going to be differences. It's believed that each prophet was sent to follow on the teachings of their predecessors and refine the message that came before, in different languages, in different eras and places. Rather than a negative, Muslims view this as a positive. Both religions highlight this as the natural progression of God's teachings to humankind, with Islam coming after Christianity, the same way Christianity refined the teachings of Judaism and prophets before Jesus."

Christian: "There has never been any natural progression of God's true teachings that diminish the supremacy of Jesus Christ."

"The Son is the image of the invisible God, the firstborn over all creation. For in him all things were created: things in heaven and on earth, visible and invisible, whether thrones or powers or rulers or authorities; all things have been created through him and for him. He is before all things, and in him all things hold together. And he is the head of the body, the church; he is the beginning and the firstborn from among the dead, so that in everything he might have the supremacy. For God was pleased to have all his fullness dwell in him, and through him to reconcile to himself all things, whether things on earth or things in heaven, by making peace through his blood, shed on the cross" (Colossians 1:15-20).

"I disbelieve any religion that denies that Jesus Christ is the Son of God, because the Bible says:

"The Father loves the Son and has placed everything in his hands. Whoever believes in the Son has eternal life, but whoever rejects the Son will not see life, for God's wrath remains on them" (John 3:35-36).

Muslim: "Muslims believe in Jesus and the other prophets as described in the Quran. This isn't to discount Islam's mandatory belief in the holy books of prophets (like the Torah and Gospel), however it's believed those books are not in their original state (via additions or subtractions) and no longer the original teachings; the Quran attempted to clarify and redress these misunderstandings."

Christian: "True Christians do not believe Mohammed's message is a continuation of our own when his message has reduced the Son of God to a mere man and prophet. While Muslims may believe in Christianity as a religion, it is clear that the teachings of Islam reject the essential teachings of Christianity as it relates to who Jesus is and how one receives salvation (forgiveness of sin) and eternal life with God."

Muslim: "I'm not very familiar on Christian teachings of forgiving sin (other than accepting Jesus as Lord and Savior). In Islam however, the general approach to sin is twofold:

1-Sins against God must be forgiven by God. This requires repenting as a (perhaps obvious) first step, but it requires a combination of faith (via prayers) and good deeds. The following I found as part of guidance (in the form of jurisprudence described above) when someone asked one of the Prophet Mohammed's companions for how to go about asking for forgiveness.

Elements of Repentance include:
1. to regret one's past evil deeds;
2. to carry out Divine duties (e.g. prayers/charity) that were missed;
3. to return the rights/properties of others that were usurped unjustly;
4. to ask forgiveness of a person whom he, has wronged, physically or verbally;
5. to make a firm resolve of avoiding the sin in future; and
6. to employ oneself in God's obedience, as he previously employed himself in God's disobedience.

2-Sins against fellow humans must be forgiven by those individuals. This is obviously meant to bring harmony in the fabric of society. So Muslims frequently ask for forgiveness from their friends/family/colleagues for wrongdoings (intentional or unintentional). Of course individuals are implored to forgive in the example of God and His Prophets."

> **"Verily, He is One Who forgives (accepts repentance), the Most Merciful."**
> **Quran 2:37**
>
> **"Those who repent, believe, and do good deeds: God will change the evil deeds of such people into good ones." Quran 25:70**

Christian: "There is common ground, as the Bible teaches us to confess and repent of our sins, ask God for His forgiveness, ask forgiveness from those we have wronged, and forgive others as God has forgiven us.

> **"If we confess our sins, he is faithful and just and will forgive us our sins and purify us from all unrighteousness" (1 John 1:9).**
>
> **"In the past God overlooked such ignorance, but now he commands all people everywhere to repent. For he has set a day when he will judge the world with justice by the man he has appointed. He has given proof of this to everyone by raising him [Jesus] from the dead" (Acts 17:30-31).**

"Bear with each other and forgive whatever grievances you may have against one another. Forgive as the Lord forgave you" (Colossians 3:13).

However, when it comes to how one is saved from our sins and given eternal life, there is a noteworthy difference between Christianity and Islam. You explained that sin against God requires faith (via prayers) and good deeds. The Bible says we are saved by God's grace through faith in Jesus Christ.

"This righteousness from God comes through faith in Jesus Christ to all who believe. There is no difference, for all have sinned and fall short of the glory of God, and are justified freely by his grace through the redemption that came by Christ Jesus" (Romans 3:22-24).

"For the wages of sin is death, but the gift of God is eternal life in Christ Jesus our Lord" (Romans 6:23).

"But because of his great love for us, God, who is rich in mercy, made us alive with Christ even when we were dead in transgressions—it is by grace you have been saved.
For it is by grace you have been saved, through faith—and this is not from yourselves, it is the gift of God not by works, so that no one can boast" (Ephesians 2:4-5, 8-9).

Notice in the verses above that eternal life in Christ and being saved by grace through faith in Christ are *gifts of God*, not something that has to be earned.

"…Everyone who calls on the name of the Lord will be saved" (Romans 10:13).

Obviously, all Christians and Muslims are to do good deeds. The difference is that Christians do not do good deeds to earn our salvation. We do not do good because we feel we have to, but because we want to out of reverence and love for God and with sincere gratitude for the sacrifice Jesus made on our behalf.

"This is how we know what love is: Jesus Christ laid down his life for us" (1 John 3:16a).

As a follower of Jesus Christ, it seems to me that if someone wanted to keep as many people as possible from the truth of who Jesus truly is and keep people from being saved of our sins and from receiving eternal life in Christ, they would try to persuade them to:

- Believe the Bible has been altered, and therefore inaccurate
- Reject Jesus as being the Son of God
- Reject Jesus as the Savior and the atoning sacrifice for the sins of the world
- Deny Jesus was crucified and rose from the dead
- Deny the trinity that God is one God in three persons, the Father, Son, and Holy Spirit
- Believe they must do good deeds to try and earn forgiveness from God

In so doing, every key foundational truth proclaimed in the Bible that is of greatest spiritual value to human beings is lost, along with the hope that accompanies it. All else in the Bible, including any common ground, becomes irrelevant.

This makes me very sad as I believe the Bible is the infallible, inspired word of God and the most reliable source of truth. I have great peace in knowing Jesus is the Son of God and the one true God, that He was crucified and rose from the dead, and is the Savior of all who place their faith in Him. So my sadness comes in knowing that people have been deceived and kept from a knowledge of God's truth. Either Christians have been deceived, or Muslims have been deceived, as we clearly do not agree on who Jesus is and how one is saved from one's sins and given eternal life. But it's not necessarily the fault of the average Muslim or average Christian. It's primarily the fault of whoever deceived people. Your thoughts and feelings?"

Muslim: "I agree that with this stark of a difference, it can be disheartening to think that one side or another is deceived, however as you said, the fault lies not so much with those who practice with good intention and faith. Our joint belief in God's mercy and forgiveness is a beacon of hope. For Muslims, almost every act, speech, or meal starts with an affirmation of this: "In the name of God: the merciful, the compassionate."

Perhaps none of us will know the truth until the Day of Judgment!"

Christian: "I believe God the Father wants His children to have assurance of His love, forgiveness, and eternal life right now, today. The following words from the Bible explain how this can happen, why believing in Jesus as the Son of God is so essential to the spiritual well-being of all people, and how anyone can experience the peace and hope that accompanies the following testimony and promise:

"We accept human testimony, but God's testimony is greater because it is the testimony of God, which he has given about his Son. Whoever believes in the Son of God accepts this testimony. Whoever does not believe God has made him out to be a liar, because they have not believed the testimony God has given about his Son. And this is the testimony: God has given us eternal life, and this life is in his Son. Whoever has the

Son has life; whoever does not have the Son of God does not have life. I write these things to you who believe in the name of the Son of God so that you may know that you have eternal life" (1 John 5:9-13).

According to the verses above, there are eternal consequences to knowing Jesus for who He truly is. There is an eternal life-changing difference between knowing Jesus as a mere man and messenger versus knowing Jesus as the Son of God, Savior and Lord of your life.

As you know, there's a lot more we could talk about, but hopefully our conversation has helped us and others to have a better understanding of what we believe and why we believe it. I must admit, it's been hard at times to know what to say and how to say it, but you know my intentions are never to offend in any way. At the same time, it is important to be very honest in stating what we believe to be true."

Muslim: "Thank you for this wonderful opportunity to learn more about Christian beliefs in forgiveness and the role of Jesus. It has been a little difficult for me, without a background in religious studies or texts. As an American of Iranian descent, I came to Islam on my own as a 19-year-old in a post-September 11th world where I was expected to know and defend a religion I was born into, but didn't really practice.

I have tried to educate myself by taking classes, reading books, and engaging with people from other religions where we built bridges and learned about the pillars that composed our spirituality and faith.

I was fortunate to meet people like you where we continue these hard conversations over 15 years later! Let's hope it continues for many more."

Christian: "Thank you for your friendship, and for taking time to engage in this conversation with me. As most Muslims believe the Quran contains God's words of truth and most Christians believe the Bible contains God's words of truth, the encouragement is for all people to take time to clearly identify their source of spiritual truth, then prayerfully and carefully evaluate the reliability of that source. As there is much more to dialogue about, our prayer is that many Muslims and Christians will engage in conversations that give one another the freedom to speak the truth as each perceives it, persevere in love for one another, despite differences, and pray for God to bring all people to a knowledge of *His truth* in answer to these questions:

Who is Jesus Christ?
How does one receive salvation (forgiveness of sin) and eternal life with God?

Then trust God with the outcome."

When they hurled their insults at him, he did not retaliate; when he suffered, he made no threats. Instead, he entrusted himself to him who judges justly.

– 1 Peter 2:23

DISCUSSION QUESTIONS
CHAPTER 7

Trust God with the Outcome

1. What are the four characteristics of a Christlike dialogue? Recall them from memory and list them here. Refer back to page 23 to check your answers and then copy the definition of *Christlike Dialogue* onto the space provided in your Journal on page 141. Memorize this definition and be prepared to share it with your group. In the weeks ahead begin to observe when you see these characteristics applied or not applied in everyday conversation and in the dialogues throughout this study.

2. Read 1 Corinthians 2:14. Most people, Christians especially, have a very strong desire to "be right" and often try to persuade others to agree with their point of view. Why could this be an unrealistic expectation? Share examples of how you have personally experienced this to be true of you or of someone who disagreed with you?

3. Read Acts 17:16-34 and answer the following questions.
   a. *Where does this dialogue take place and who is present? (vv. 16-21)*

   b. *How does Paul affirm these people, establish common ground and avoid an argumentative debate? (vv. 22-23, 28)*

   c. *What truths did Paul convey? (vv. 24-31)*

d. What was the outcome of the dialogue and how did Paul trust God with the outcome? (vv. 32-34)

4. In your discussion group, have two people read the dialogue between the Muslim and the Christian aloud. Discuss your observations of the dialogue. What characteristics and guidelines of *Christlike Dialogue* did you see being practiced?

5. On a scale of 0 to 5, rate yourself on the following scale. Discuss the results with your group. If you are a 5, why? If you are not a 5, why not?

0   1   2   3   4   5

I try to control the outcome and don't   *I trust God with the outcome*
trust God in all situations/conversations.   *in all situations/conversations.*

....

GUIDELINE FOCUS: **FIND COMMON GROUND**

IDENTIFY A COMMON SUBJECT OF INTEREST FOR THE DIALOGUE. READ JOHN 4:1-26 FOR AN EXAMPLE. IT CAN BE ANYTHING YOU CAN IDENTIFY AS COMMON GROUND (SUCH AS WATER IN THE EXAMPLE) THAT MIGHT HELP YOU RELATE TO ONE ANOTHER MORE CLEARLY.

What have you learned from the examples of common ground in John 4:1-26 and Acts 17:16-34 that will help you engage in a Christlike dialogue? Review the testimony you wrote for Chapter 6 on page 140 of your Journal and consider the person/people God laid on your heart. Pray for a deeper connection. Can you identify any common ground between you and this/these other person/people? Note this in your Journal in Appendix B on page 141.

APPLICATION

Perhaps the person you identified in Chapter 6 is a Muslim, or someone else of another faith. Maybe your friend is an atheist. Ask them if they would be open to having a spiritual conversation with you to learn what you both believe about who Jesus is, and how each of you came to believe as you do. Share the guidelines for Christlike dialogue and ask if they agree to abide by them. Make it clear you are not meeting to debate. You simply want to engage in conversation to learn from and better understand what you both believe and why you believe as you do. You can share from the testimony that you prepared in Chapter 6 and ask the other person to tell their story, perhaps prompting them with some of the questions the panel members were asked in Chapter 6 and/or those listed on page 79 and below:

- What common ground do you share?
- What is your understanding of who Jesus is?
- How does a person receive forgiveness of sins and eternal life with God?
- What happens after we die?
- How would you describe the Bible and its purpose?
- How did you come to believe what you believe?
- What is your source of truth upon which you base your answers?
- Is your source of truth reliable? If yes, what do you base that on?
- How certain are you that what you believe is true?

Remember to leave the outcome of this dialogue with God.

From your conversation, what did you learn? Make some notes on page 141 of your Journal in Appendix B.

CHAPTER 8

THE MEEK SURRENDER, BUT NEVER LOSE

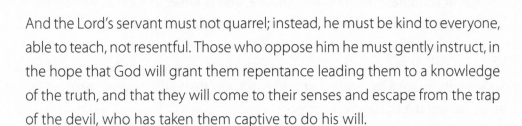

And the Lord's servant must not quarrel; instead, he must be kind to everyone, able to teach, not resentful. Those who oppose him he must gently instruct, in the hope that God will grant them repentance leading them to a knowledge of the truth, and that they will come to their senses and escape from the trap of the devil, who has taken them captive to do his will.

– 2 Timothy 2:24-26

High on my list of favorite Scriptures are Jesus' words in Matthew 11:28-30: "Come to me, all you who are weary and burdened, and I will give you rest. Take my yoke upon you and learn from me, for I am gentle and humble in heart, and you will find rest for your souls. For my yoke is easy and my burden light." …What does He mean, to take His yoke? …Where is rest hiding?

The answer lies in meekness. In this passage, Christ calls Himself "gentle and humble"— meek. He came not to judge but to die. He came not to shout and defend the honor of the Father but to die. He came not to fight but to die. No persecution could disturb Him for He came to suffer. Yet all the time He was suffering, He knew He was winning.

We, too, can suffer and win. We can live with love even when others hate—all the time knowing that love wins. We can respond with grace when others fight, knowing that grace wins. When we come to Him and surrender, accepting His yoke, we accept full vulnerability to the onslaught of the world. Yet, at the same time, we are assured that nothing can separate us from the victorious love of Christ. This rest is a self-weakening unto God-strength. It is a self-emptying unto God-fullness. It is the rest of full surrender.

Jesus calls us to His rest, and meekness is His method.

—Richard A. Swenson, M.D., *Margin*, pp. 233-234

WHAT MUST WE SURRENDER?

What "self-emptying" must take place if we are to rest in full surrender to God? The answer begins with a willingness to correct the wrong use of words we speak. James, the half-brother of Jesus understood the significance and need for taming our tongues when he wrote:

"We all stumble in many ways. Anyone who is never at fault in what they say is perfect, able to keep their whole body in check" (James 3:2).

Think about that! The Word of God is saying that if we are never at fault in what we say, we've arrived and are fully mature in Christ. We know that none of us are never at fault in what we say, yet the challenge is there.

One way to consider "self-emptying" involves giving up our right to be "right". There is a very strong powerful drive within humans to be right. But when being "right" takes priority over persevering in love for people despite differences, we need to be willing to give up our right to be "right". Please remember; this does not mean we compromise truth or stop doing what is right. It does mean we stop trying to persuade people to see things exactly as we do.

Another way we can model the meekness of Christ, this "self-emptying", as it relates to the way we respond to people who see things differently than we do, is by heeding the three "musts" Paul outlines in 2 Timothy 2:24-25:

- *We must not quarrel.*
- *We must be kind to everyone.*
- *We must gently instruct others.*

Our obedience to this instruction releases the power of the Holy Spirit to touch hearts in ways that bring conviction of sin and an openness to the truth. Many in our society perceive meekness as weakness, and yet meekness is the greatest strength we can have. In fact, obedience to 2 Timothy 2:24-25 requires meekness. Consider Jesus as He prayed in Gethsemane before His imminent crucifixion and death:

"Father, if you are willing, take this cup from me; yet not my will, but yours be done" (Luke 22:42).

That's meekness; humble, absolute surrender to the will of God, regardless of the cost!

If you are in the midst of a disagreement with someone, and want to know if you are willing to take Jesus' yoke by surrendering to the will and ways of God, ask yourself these questions:

- Am I refraining from quarreling with this person?
- Am I being kind to this human being?
- Am I gently instructing this individual?

Do you have the love of Christ for that person? Do you have concern for Christ's interests and the spiritual well-being of the person with a differing view? Or, do you simply have anger and resentment toward him or her because they are getting in the way of your self-interests?

To those who recognize and acknowledge they have fallen short of responding to opposition in ways that glorify God, I encourage you to practice Christlike dialogue when responding to and communicating with people of opposing views—people you may perceive to be your enemy—yet people God has allowed into your life for a reason.

As you talk with non-Christians who disagree with you about controversial issues, remember these words:

"The man without the Spirit does not accept the things that come from the Spirit of God, for they are foolishness to him, and he cannot understand them, because they are spiritually discerned" (1 Corinthians 2:14).

If the opposing party is not a Christian, are you open to sharing the gospel with the person as the Holy Spirit leads you to? Will you pray for that person's salvation?

Even if your concern is legitimate, we must never forget how patient God has been with us so that we do not become impatient with others.

While we must never stop doing what is right, let us remember that others may not yet have the spiritual understanding and power to do so.

THE LORD'S SERVANT MUST NOT QUARREL

Arguing may be okay but quarreling isn't. The *Oxford American Dictionary* includes the following definitions for the words, "argue" and "quarrel":

Argue: To give reasons for or against something, to debate.
Quarrel: A violent disagreement, breaking of friendly relations.

Arguing might be okay when it's simply a discussion of a particular issue or matter of concern like discussing a business decision. But not all arguing is okay, as Paul points out in 2 Timothy 2:23, *Don't have anything to do with stupid and foolish arguments, because you know they produce quarrels.*

At the point of disagreement when one or both parties begin to break off friendly relations with one another, the discussion moves from arguing to quarreling, *and the Lord's servant must not quarrel.*

If you have feelings of resentment toward someone else's opinion, and also toward that person, be careful. **You are at risk of focusing more on the issue than the relationship if your motive to be "right" takes priority over the motive of love for the other person.** If Satan can cause you to have bitterness and hatred toward another person, he's succeeding at influencing you to represent Jesus poorly.

Our motivations provide the focus for conversation. What is my motive? Is my motive to "be right" on this issue, or to "do right" for this relationship?

THE LORD'S SERVANT MUST BE KIND TO EVERYONE

From 1993 through 2001, God blessed my sons and me with what I refer to as our "tent making" business, similar to the apostle Paul. Rather than make tents, we had an independent insurance claims adjusting business. We subcontracted work from insurance companies in Denver to adjust property claims for homeowners. Most of the claims we adjusted involved hail damage to roofs.

One summer I received a telephone call from a supervisor of an insurance company we serviced. He explained that an insured had called and was quite upset with the insurance claims adjuster who recently inspected his property. The homeowner thought the adjuster was rude and unreasonable and he didn't understand why his claim was denied. He wanted a second opinion. The supervisor asked if I would be willing to re-inspect the property. I agreed to and telephoned the insured to make an appointment.

Normally, in scheduling our days, my sons and I spent around fifteen minutes or so to inspect a property and assess the damage. Knowing this man was upset, I cleared our schedule so I could take as much time as needed to hear his concerns.

After meeting the insured, we began the inspection. He had a long list of damage of which he wanted me to take note. He began by showing me damage to the paint on the sides of

Is my motive to "BE RIGHT" on this issue,

or to "DO RIGHT" for this relationship?

his home. The paint was bubbling up and peeling, so I calmly explained that the damage was a result of deterioration of the paint and not the result of hail damage. Next, he pointed out window screens that were wearing out. I politely showed him that the screens on all four sides of the house had similar damage, including screens that were well protected from hail by an overhang. He then understood that the damage was due to the screens being old, and not caused by the hail. When we inspected the roof, he identified extensive damage to the composition shingles. Patiently, I explained that when hail causes scarring and granule loss to that type of roof, noticeable indentations can usually be found on the back of the shingles and fresh bright black marks on the front of the shingles indicating the damage is recent. So he could actually see for himself, I took time to show him that there were no indentations and that the granule loss from the shingles had left them gray, not black. I further explained that the evidence confirmed that the damage was from deterioration of the shingles since they only turn gray from sun exposure over time. After spending four hours with the gentleman, I gently informed him that his claim would be denied.

The man looked me in the eyes and said, "I want to thank you for your kindness."

I replied, "You are welcome", and immediately thought to myself, *That wasn't my kindness. That was the* **kindness of Christ in me.**

PREPARING OUR HEARTS

God, through His Holy Spirit and Word, had been teaching me to **embrace conflict as an opportunity to grow in my knowledge of His Son**, and to respond to others as He would.

That, together with the insurance supervisor's warning about the insured's feelings, kept me from being caught off guard. The time I had to align my heart and mind with the Spirit of Christ was helpful.

But what if I hadn't been forewarned? Instead, let's say my sons and I had planned a typical day of adjusting property claims, with ten appointments scheduled, allowing roughly one hour per claim, including travel time and at our sixth appointment we were unexpectedly confronted with the dissatisfied insured. Would I have been as **patient**, knowing we had four more appointments? Would I have been as **kind**, realizing that people might get upset if we were late or needed to reschedule? Would I have responded with the fruit of Christ's Spirit, or might I have responded in the flesh by being impatient and unkind? The answer would depend on whether or not I decided that day and that moment to abide in Christ and walk in His Spirit, fully surrendered to Him, and prepared to respond with the heart and mind of Jesus.

What about *you*? Will you be walking close enough with Christ to respond with the fruit of His Spirit, or will you be at risk of using words that displease God and don't reflect His character? All of us encounter people who irritate us and disrupt our otherwise comfortable daily routine. What action will you take to prepare your heart for such an encounter?

THE LORD'S SERVANT MUST GENTLY INSTRUCT

In the following scenario a father and his eighteen-year-old son have a difference of opinion.

The son, away at his first year of college calls home and asks his father what he thinks about him getting a tattoo. The father tries to discourage his son from getting a tattoo, then both drop the subject. A couple of weeks later, the son comes home for spring break sporting a new tattoo. His mom is out of town to care for her aging mother, so this is to be a special father and son time together. In the two conversations that follow, note the difference in outcome between harsh words and gentle instruction.

FIRST CONVERSATION: FATHER AND SON

The first conversation involves two monologues. The scenario unfolds as the son's car pulls into the driveway. The father is at the front door to greet him, but as he spots the tattoo, his smile turns to a scowl. He is very upset, and responds harshly. His son becomes defensive.

Father: "Well look at you! I thought I told you not to get that tattoo. What's wrong with you?"

Son: "Dad, all my friends have one. We don't see anything wrong with it."

Father: "Well, your generation doesn't see a lot of things that are wrong. When I was your age, none of my friends or I ever had a tattoo. "

Son: "Maybe so, but your generation did a lot of other things that were wrong. If your generation hadn't been so messed up, maybe ours wouldn't be either."

Father: "You don't talk that way to me, young man. The bottom line is that if you're going to live in this house, you'll live by my rules. I'm the one who's paying for your college. Unless you want to pay yourself, you'll do as I tell you."

Son: "Look, I chose to come home over spring break to spend some time with you and go fishing like you said. But you know what? Sam said I could go camping with him and his family, so I'm outta here. Sorry I ever came." (Son picks up unpacked bags and slams the door on his way out.)

SECOND CONVERSATION: FATHER AND SON

As you read this second conversation, observe the words and implied heart attitudes again. The details remain the same, but the Holy Spirit has prepared the heart and mind of the father to respond to his son in a more Christlike way—with **gentle instruction**.

As his son's car pulls into the driveway, the father hurries to the door to greet him. Although he notices his son's tattoo, he gives him a big hug.

Father: "Welcome home, son. It's great to see you. How was your drive home? The coals are hot, and the steaks will be ready whenever you are."

Son: (Returning his father's hug) "Great! I'm starving. Let me dump this stuff, and I'll be right out."

After listening to his son share about his classes and friends at college over dinner, the conversation resumes.

Father: "Ready for some strawberry shortcake?"

Son: "Yeah, that sounds awesome."

Father: "I see that you decided to get a tattoo after all. Did it hurt?"

Son: "It did hurt, Dad. I know you tried to talk me out of getting this, but my buddies and I just thought it would be kinda fun if we all got one."

Father: "Although I am old school and don't approve of the tattoo, I want you to know that there's nothing you could do that would ever cause me to stop loving you."

Son: "Thanks, Dad. I love you too."

Father: "May I share something with you?"

Son: "Sure, Dad."

Father: "I realize you are at an age where your decisions should be between you and God, but you asked for my advice. And it really hurt me when you ignored my counsel."

Son: "I didn't mean to hurt you, Dad. I didn't think I ignored you. I remember you tried to discourage me, but you never told me *not* to get the tattoo. I figured it was my choice. I'm eighteen now."

Father: "That's true son; and that's my fault. I should have taken more time initially to ask why you wanted the tattoo, and to listen more closely to your response. I was wrong for not praying with you about it."

Son: "Dad, it's my fault, too. I probably wasn't listening to you because I really wanted the tattoo. I know you've taught me to pray first about all decisions, and to wait patiently for God's answers, but I didn't want to wait. I see now that I just wanted my own way. I'm sorry if my actions have hurt you, and if they have hurt God. I will pray and ask God to forgive me. Will you forgive me? I do respect you, Dad."

Father: "Son, I do forgive you. The tattoo isn't the issue. What's of concern, is your heart and your character, and you just proved to God and me that both your heart and character are just fine. I'm blessed to have you for a son. I'm sorry, too. I really didn't take sufficient time to really listen and talk with you when you first mentioned the possibility of getting a tattoo. Will you forgive me? C'mon, let's pray together, okay?"

Son: "I do forgive you, and would love to pray with you, Dad."

Father and son pray together with the father asking for forgiveness for not being fully available to his son to mentor him in this decision process with God.

Father: "I sure do love you, son."

A CHANGE OF HEART

How does the second conversation differ from the first? How do the following verses apply?

> **"A gentle answer turns away wrath, but a harsh word stirs up anger" (Proverbs 15:1).**

> **"Fathers, do not provoke your children, lest they become discouraged" (Colossians 3:21, ESV).**

> **"Always be humble and gentle. Be patient with each other, making allowance for each other's faults because of your love" (Ephesians 4:2, NLT).**

Prior to the second conversation, the gentle whisper of the Holy Spirit may have uttered some convicting questions for the father to ponder, such as:

- Have there been times in your life when your heavenly Father made it clear to you that it wasn't His will for you to do something, but you did it anyway?
- Did God patiently bear with you, extending His grace by giving you time to repent and mature without withdrawing His love for you?
- How is God wanting to conform you to the likeness of His Son through this disagreement with your child?

May these father/son conversations serve to remind us that harsh words facilitate two monologues at best. Gentle instruction, on the other hand reflects maturity in Christ and smooths the way for the building of close relationships.

And the Lord's servant must not quarrel; instead, he must be kind to everyone, able to teach, not resentful. Those who oppose him he must gently instruct, in the hope that God will grant them repentance leading them to a knowledge of the truth, and that they will come to their senses and escape from the trap of the devil, who has taken them captive to do his will.

– 2 Timothy 2:24-26

DISCUSSION QUESTIONS
CHAPTER 8

The Meek Surrender, But Never Lose

1. *The Lord's servant must not quarrel.* Read Acts 15:36-41. Paul and Barnabas loved the Lord, but they had a sharp disagreement over whether or not to take Barnabas' cousin, John Mark, on another missionary journey with them because John Mark had deserted them on an earlier missionary journey. They parted company because of the disagreement. How could Paul and Barnabas have responded in God-honoring ways to the situation, without quarreling?

2. *The Lord's servant must be kind to everyone.* How would you demonstrate kindness in a conversation with someone who has a viewpoint or belief that opposes your value system? Give examples. Would any of these examples differ in any ways from your previous approaches to a conflict with someone? Read your response to Discussion Question 1 in Chapter Two on page 25. What might change and why would it?

3. *The Lord's servant must gently instruct.* In what ways is the second conversation between the father and son an example of gentle instruction?

4. Read 2 Timothy 2:23. How would you define a stupid and foolish argument? Write down a few examples of instances you have experienced or heard about in which arguments have led to strife and division within a congregation, between denominations, at home, or in the workplace.

5. Identify a meek/humble person you know and consider what makes them seem meek/humble. In your group discuss one or two of these people and on page 142 of your Journal in Appendix B list the common characteristics of people that exhibit this quality.

GUIDELINE FOCUS: **BE HUMBLE**

IF ONE OF THE PARTIES IS IN AUTHORITY OVER THE OTHER(S), IT'S IMPORTANT TO GIVE PEOPLE UNDER AUTHORITY FREEDOM TO RESPECTFULLY DISCUSS MATTERS OF CONCERN WITHOUT NEGATIVE CONSEQUENCES.

Look up, Matthew 20:25-28, the verse on which this guideline is based, and copy it into your Journal in Appendix B on page 142.

APPLICATION

This week spend some time pondering (perhaps even doing a little deeper Bible study) on what it truly means for every human being to be created in the image of God; this includes any individual God has allowed into your life who might hurt and aggravate you in any number of ways. Perhaps for you, this individual is not someone you consider an "enemy", but instead, is someone under your authority who just doesn't seem to ever get things "right" or do them the same way you would. Is it someone at work or perhaps a son, daughter, spouse or mother-in-law?

Read and meditate on Genesis 1:27 and James 3:9-10; then write out a prayer asking God to give you eyes to see this person through Jesus' eyes. Copy your prayer into your Journal in Appendix B on page 143. If you have been harsh with anyone, go to that person and ask for their forgiveness.

CHAPTER 9

PERSEVERE IN LOVE, DESPITE DIFFERENCES

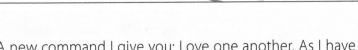

A new command I give you: Love one another. As I have loved you, so you must love one another. By this all men will know that you are my disciples, if you love one another.

– John 13:34-35

CHRISTIAN UNITY AND THE 2016 PRESIDENTIAL ELECTION
…There has never in my lifetime been so much division among Christians around a presidential campaign. But the candidacy of Donald Trump has created a massive amount of division. That line of division is drawn between Christians who say they will never vote for Trump and Christians who say we must vote for Trump.

But my concern…is not first who Americans would elect to be their next president. My concern this week is whether Christians can love one another well when the election is over.

– Heath Lambert, November 7, 2016 edition of *Truth in Love*

The two conversations that follow are between two Christians. The first conversation takes place just prior to the 2016 presidential election between Donald Trump and Hillary Clinton.

FIRST CONVERSATION: AN AFRICAN AMERICAN DEMOCRAT AND A WHITE REPUBLICAN

Democrat: "Why would any Christian vote for Donald Trump? He's racist, has a history of womanizing and adultery, uses offensive language, lacks integrity and is only about money and power."

Republican: "Why would any Christian vote for Hillary Clinton? She is pro-abortion, and lacks respect for religious liberty. If elected, she will add justices to the Supreme Court who will support the liberal agenda for many years to come. She's a career politician who appears to care, but only when it will help her get the votes of the people who are listening. I think she is just as much about the money and power as Donald Trump is. It's obvious she prefers socialism to democracy because it gives greater power to the government to direct and control the lives of average citizens."

Democrat: "So you know Hillary pretty well, huh? When's the last time you met and had a conversation with her? My point is that I question whether Trump is even a Christian, so why would Christians vote for him?"

Republican: "Do you think it was right when some white people questioned whether or not President Obama was a Christian? Who were they to judge him, and who are you to judge whether or not Trump is a Christian? What does that have to do with being president anyway? If you needed surgery, would you prefer a poor surgeon who is a Christian, or an excellent surgeon who is not a Christian?"

Democrat: "We're not talking about surgery, we're talking about someone representing our nation as president. Trump has already offended and will continue to offend a lot of people, including leaders of other countries. And it's not just black people who are concerned, but also Hispanic immigrants and Muslims. He doesn't appear to be an advocate for minorities."

Republican: "Well, I think there are a lot of Americans who are fed up with the typical politicians who have proven to be very incompetent. At least Trump has quite a bit of business experience that can help government programs operate more efficiently, and he will see that the United States is no longer taken advantage of when it comes to foreign trade."

Democrat: "Trump has been a successful businessman, but has he been an honest businessman? I question his integrity."

Republican: "Are politicians known for being honest and having integrity? Are they known for being competent? If so, why does the US Postal Service lose billions of dollars in a year but continue to operate in the same way? Why is our national debt in the trillions? Why would we ever borrow money from a communist country, as we have? We need a change in leadership."

Democrat: "I still don't understand why any Christian would vote for Trump."

Republican: "I still don't understand why any Christian would vote for Clinton."

Did you hear a Christlike dialogue? Were they other-minded, or did they have selfish ambition? Do you think each person was slow to speak and quick to listen?

What did that conversation accomplish, other than two people expressing their **opinions**? Were those opinions based upon facts and truth, or just what each perceived to be true?

Was there any focus on how God might want to use their disagreement to help them know Christ better? Did they represent Jesus well through the words they spoke to one another?

Do you think they had peace in the midst of this conflict because they trusted God with the outcome, or were they both trying to be "right", win the argument, and control the outcome?

IT'S A SPIRITUAL BATTLE

May we never forget how real the spiritual battle is between good and evil.

> **"Finally, be strong in the Lord and in His mighty power. Put on the full armor of God so that you can take your stand against the devil's schemes. For our struggle is not against flesh and blood, but against the rulers, against the authorities, against the powers of this dark world and against the spiritual forces of evil in the heavenly realms" (Ephesians 6:10-12).**

With each disagreement, Satan is at work trying to cause hatred and division. His goal is to have people get so upset with the opposition, that they withdraw their love for each other. At the same time, the Holy Spirit gently reminds us to persevere in our love for one another, despite differences.

Satan's strategy is to deceive people into believing these two lies:

1. **Issues are more important than relationships.**
2. **Being "right" is more important than doing right.**

There is a strong desire within human beings to be right and get our way. So when someone comes along who doesn't see things exactly as we do, with the potential to keep us from getting our way, our sinful hearts and spiritual immaturity are often revealed.

The choice is always ours to make. We can choose to be "right", or we can choose to do right.

To do right is to persevere in love for people, despite differences.

- **That does not mean we condone or agree with something that is wrong.**
- **It does not mean we compromise truth, or stop doing what is right.**
- **But it does mean we stop trying to get people to see things exactly as we do.**

We need to guard against feelings of anger, resentment, or ill-will toward another person. Those feelings should be a red flag that signal a warning, alerting us to the risk of being deceived and of withdrawing our love for that person. May we encourage one another to obey Christ's command to love others as He has loved us (John 13:34), and not allow issues of concern to take precedence.

When God allows circumstances where we find ourselves in disagreement with someone, it is extremely important to remember that our struggle is not actually with that person. Our energy should not be directed at avoiding the conflict or at being "right" and getting our way. Instead, we should ask God how He wants to use the disagreement to help us know Him better, become more like His Son, and represent Jesus well in conversations that are honoring to God.

Ask God how He wants to use the disagreement to

HELP YOU KNOW HIM BETTER.

SECOND CONVERSATION: AN AFRICAN AMERICAN DEMOCRAT AND A WHITE REPUPLICAN

The election is over and the new president is Donald Trump. Two brothers in Christ engage in a Christlike dialogue to discuss the results and prayerfully consider how to move forward.

Democrat: "A survey has shown that 80% of Evangelical Christians voted for Trump. Many of those votes came from districts in the suburbs where the population is predominantly white. The majority of black people view Hillary Clinton as more of an advocate for civil rights, than President Trump. We feel as though the racial divide that exists in America is of little concern to our white brothers and sisters in Christ."

Republican: "I don't know of any Christian who voted for Trump because they are opposed to civil rights. The people I know who voted for Trump, voted for him only because they thought he was the better choice between two poor options."

Democrat: "Is the fact that she is pro-abortion the only reason people prefer Trump over Clinton?"

Republican: "No. That is one primary concern, but there are other reasons. One is that Hillary seems to prefer socialism to democracy. Let me explain where this reasoning comes from. I've read that there are various levels of control that are important to creating a social state. Here are a few examples:

- Healthcare – control healthcare and you can control the people.
- Education – take control of what people read and listen to, especially what children learn in school.
- Religion – remove the belief in God from the government and schools.
- Gun control – remove the ability to defend themselves from the government. That way you are able to create a police state.

Many would say Hillary favors these levels of government control, plus others I've not mentioned. Shouldn't American voters be opposed to candidates who favor a social state over a republic, the republic America has always been?"

Democrat: "Not if the alternative increases the spread of racism in America. I realize this is difficult for my white friends to understand because the ancestors of their race did not experience 400 years of slavery in this country, and most white people are unaffected by the racial injustice that still exists in America."

Republican: "I believe it's true that most white people in America are ignorant of and insensitive to racial injustice and lack empathy for our black brothers and sisters. Most of us have not personally experienced racial injustice, and we are mostly unaffected by it. It's difficult for us to relate to. That's why it's important to engage in conversations like this. Maybe we can gain understanding and see the situation more clearly from your perspective. Do you view racism and racial injustice as a greater sin than abortion?"

Democrat: "There are no unborn children who have fear of white supremacy, but there are many black people who do. The reality of the atrocities, the hurt, the pain, the unimaginable suffering, the sadness, the fear, the injustice of those 400 years are not easily erased with time. Couple that with the fact that racism is still prevalent in America, and you can begin to see from our perspective why it matters to us who you vote for."

Republican: "That helps me understand your perspective a lot more and I'm sorry our nation allowed slavery at all, let alone permitted it to continue for 400 years. It was atrocious sin and any racism that exists today is awful and needs to be repented of. That said, many of our white brothers and sisters believe just as strongly that taking the life of an innocent baby has always been a terrible sin that needs to end. It doesn't just affect the lives of the unborn child, but also has serious negative consequences for women who have had abortions, many of whom are Christians. So as Christians, black or white, Republican or Democrat, which of the following do you think God would want us to give highest priority to?

- Ending racism
- Ending abortion
- Persevering in love for one another, despite differences

Democrat: "To persevere in love for one another, as Jesus said":

"A new command I give you: Love one another. As I have loved you, so you must love one another. By this, all men will know that you are my disciples, if you love one another" (John 13:34-35).

Martin Luther King, Jr. made this statement:

I know that love is ultimately the only answer to mankind's problems...

Republican: "I would love to continue to meet and engage in further conversation. If you would as well, can you think of three African American friends who might like to join us? I'd be glad to invite three white friends. As a *Group of Eight*, we can make a commitment to meet and discuss racial concerns in America."

Democrat: "Let's pray about that. Dear God, thank you for this conversation with my brother. We ask you to bring these eight people together to engage in conversations about race and racial tensions in America in ways that are honoring to you. In Jesus' name, amen."

A new command I give you: Love one another. As I have loved you, so you must love one another. By this all men will know that you are my disciples, if you love one another.

– John 13:34-35

DISCUSSION QUESTIONS
CHAPTER 9

Persevere in Love, Despite Differences

1. In what ways did the two men represent Jesus poorly in the first conversation?

2. In what ways did the two men represent Jesus well in the second conversation?

3. Read the section on IT'S A SPIRITUAL BATTLE on page 109. Discuss the spiritual battle between good and evil, and how this battle takes place when differences arise. Give examples from the following areas of life: marriage, parenting, workplace, church, race, religion, and politics.

4. Think about a few situations where it has been difficult to persevere in love for other Christians. Plan to discuss a couple of these with your group.

5. What are your thoughts about forming or participating in a *Group of Eight* where people with differing views engage in conversations that honor God? For more information about forming a *Group of Eight*, visit ChristlikeDialogue.org.

....

GUIDELINE FOCUS: **PERSEVERE IN LOVE, DESPITE DIFFERENCES**

IT IS NOT IMPORTANT TO AGREE WITH ONE ANOTHER; IT IS IMPORTANT THAT YOU EXTEND MUTUAL RESPECT, AVOID QUARRELING, AND BE CONSIDERATE OF OTHERS, DESPITE DIFFERENCES. THIS DOES NOT MEAN THAT YOU CONDONE SOMETHING YOU BELIEVE IS WRONG, BUT IT DOES MEAN THAT YOU DON'T WITHDRAW YOUR LOVE FROM

OTHERS JUST BECAUSE THEY DON'T SEE THINGS EXACTLY AS YOU DO. REMEMBER: THE RELATIONSHIP IS MORE IMPORTANT THAN THE ISSUE. (JOHN 13:34-35; TITUS 3:1-2)

Look up John 13:34-35; Titus 3:1-2, the verses on which this guideline is based, and copy them into your Journal in Appendix B on page 144.

APPLICATION

As you have been completing this study, how has God spoken to your heart? Has he prompted you to heal a broken relationship through the miracle of dialogue? Has He laid a particular group of people or current divisive issue on your heart? How is God challenging you to *Persevere in Love, Despite Differences*?

One way to engage in this mission is to start and participate in a *Group of Eight* to discuss differences. This week, take some time to visit ChristlikeDialogue.org to learn more about starting a *Group of Eight*.

Perhaps you would gather a group of people to discuss racial concerns, gender issues, generational differences, challenges within the workplace, another matter of concern, or form a group to discuss faith questions. Ask God to show you where He is challenging you to *Persevere in Love, Despite Differences* in your relationships with others, and be prepared to share with your group. Do others in your small group want to choose a topic and continue to meet and invite others into the conversation?

As one example, if you form a group to explore faith questions, your group would consist of four Christians and four people who are not yet Christians. You might begin by asking the non-Christians what they think about Christians, and why. Sharing your stories is very helpful and powerful in connecting people to one another. You could continue the conversation by selecting thought-provoking questions similar to the ones shared in Chapter 6 with the panel of non-Christians. For additional resources for a *Group of Eight*, that consists of Christians and non-Christians, visit QPlace.com and ExploreGod.com.

As you intentionally engage in Christlike dialogue with others, always remember to *Persevere in Love, Despite Differences*.

Record your action step in the space provided on page 144 of your Journal in Appendix B.

CHAPTER 10

FROM DEBATE TO
CHRISTLIKE DIALOGUE

Let the words of my mouth and the meditation of my heart be acceptable in your sight, O LORD, my rock and my redeemer.

– Psalm 19:14, ESV

Every man is a potential adversary, even those whom we love. Only through dialogue are we saved from this enmity toward one another. Dialogue is to love, what blood is to the body. When the flow of blood stops, the body dies. When dialogue stops, love dies and resentment and hate are born. But dialogue can restore a dead relationship. Indeed, this is the miracle of dialogue: it can bring relationship into being, and it can bring into being once again a relationship that has died.

There is only one qualification to these claims for dialogue: it must be mutual and proceed from both sides, and the parties to it must persist relentlessly. The word of dialogue may be spoken by one side but evaded or ignored by the other, in which case the promise may not be fulfilled. There is risk in speaking the dialogical word—that is, in entering into dialogue—but when two persons undertake it and accept their fear of doing so, the miracle-working power of dialogue may be released.

—Reuel L. Howe, *The Miracle of Dialogue*, pp. 3-4

In defining debate, two words come to mind: *argue* and *dispute*. Two words that help define dialogue are: *conversation* and *talk*. I don't know about you, but I sense some tension in the words, *argue* and *dispute* that disappears with the words, *conversation* and *talk*. To go a step further, it's important to note a significant difference between dialogue and Christlike dialogue. With dialogue, self-interests may still exist, but with true Christlike dialogue, selfish ambition is replaced with a sincere desire to focus on Christ's primary interests, which include:

- **Salvation** – for people to believe in and receive Jesus as their Savior and Lord.
- **Sanctification** – for Christians to obey Jesus as Lord and become more like Him.

Study the following chart to identify significant differences between debate and Christlike dialogue.

	DEBATE	**CHRISTLIKE DIALOGUE**
GOAL	Win the argument	Represent Jesus well for God's glory
MOTIVE	To be "right"	To do right by persevering in love for people, despite differences
KNOWLEDGE	Used to prove point and persuade others to agree with you	Use humbly to point people to Jesus and the Word of God
LISTENING	Only to counter opposing views	To gain a better understanding of what others believe, and why they believe it

KEEPING IT SIMPLE

We encourage you to initiate dialogue in the simplest way possible. In the introduction of this study guide, I explained how I initiated dialogue with the leader of a secular organization in regard to sex education in the public schools. I simply called her on the phone and asked if she would be willing to meet with me to dialogue. I explained that my purpose was to see if we could find some common ground and learn together where we disagreed. She accepted my offer and we met and agreed that our common ground was "healthier kids and a healthy society". We decided when and how often we would meet, and then began to dialogue.

Initiating dialogue can be as simple as asking someone if they are willing to dialogue about a concern you have. If the answer is "Yes", you have begun.

After attending a seminar on *Christlike Dialogue*, a woman initiated dialogue with her sister. One is a Democrat; the other a Republican. She wrote:

> *This seminar made me realize that I didn't have to win or change my mind or the other person's mind in order to have a conversation. I also didn't have to lose. It opened me to asking questions and getting another point of view rather than having an agenda.*
>
> *I found conversing with people now is a lot more fun, and I can get involved in a conversation where I know people are not on the same side as me. I'm finding that really interesting, and it's stretching me. With this approach, I'm also finding some common ground—for two reasons. First, I'm involved in a conversation that I wouldn't have had, and second, I'm not approaching it as an antagonist. That helps people listen to me because I'm listening to them. It's not magic; it just feels like it. So different than before. Instead of always being on edge with my sister, I was able to relax and just enjoy all the good things about her. That critical spirit that was often around when we were together wasn't there this time. Instead, it was a spirit of affirmation.*

I urge you to keep in mind the fact that people are at different levels of spiritual maturity. Check the expectations you have of yourself or others to be sure they are realistic. You're not there to change the person to your way of thinking. Remain humble, teachable and open to patiently bearing with others in love. Allow time for the Holy Spirit to work in people's lives, including yours.

Prepare to respond as Christ would, but be equally prepared for others not to. Remember that discussing differences of opinion often reveals hearts and how much we have, or have not, grown in grace.

Grace is the undeserved love of God for sinners like you and me, expressed through His mercy, kindness and forgiveness of sins made possible by the crucifixion and resurrection of His Son to all who place their faith in the Lord Jesus Christ. As children of God, there may be occasion to extend this same kind of grace to people who we might perceive to be undeserving of our love. Is the Holy Spirit nudging you to extend grace to someone today?

GUIDELINES FOR CHRISTLIKE DIALOGUE

The following guidelines are designed for equipping people to initiate and engage in a Christlike dialogue with someone who has an opposing view. They help to establish parameters for the people involved in the conversation, but they are not offered as steps that everyone must follow. The primary purpose of these guidelines is to prepare hearts for Christlike dialogue.

1. **PRAY.** Ask God to help you gain a greater understanding of each other, of what is true, and of what God might want to reveal about Himself through the conversation.

   "As for God, his way is perfect; the word of the Lord is flawless. He is a shield for all who take refuge in him" (Psalm 18:30).

   Prayer is essential to Christlike dialogue if the true desire of our hearts is to discover how God wants to use disagreements to help us know Jesus better and become more like Him.

   "Search me, O God, and know my heart; test me and know my anxious thoughts. See if there is any offensive way in me, and lead me in the way everlasting" (Psalm 139:23-24).

   As you pray, ask God to give you His perspective so you represent Jesus well by practicing other-minded listening, seeking and speaking the truth in love, focusing on Christ's interests, and trusting God with the outcome.

2. **FIND COMMON GROUND.** Identify a common subject of interest for the dialogue. Read John 4:1-26 for an example. It can be anything you identify as common ground (such as water in the example) that might help you relate to one another more clearly.

   To learn more about the importance of identifying common ground and using it as a means of building bridges, read John 21:15-22.

   If the disagreement is between two Christians, the common ground might be a mutual desire to mature in Christ and learn what God may have to teach each of you while discussing differences.

   Going back to the conversations in Chapter Nine, the dialogue parties were different in race and political views, yet they found common ground as brothers in Christ with a like-minded desire for unity and a mutual willingness to persevere in love for one another, despite differences.

3. **BE HONEST.** Authenticity is highly valued.

   My wife Candy and I serve in the ministry of *Starting Point* at our church. *Starting Point* is designed to be a conversational environment in which people explore faith and experience community. It's a great opportunity for us to practice Christlike dialogue.

   I will never forget serving as facilitators on the first day with our first group. We were going around the circle with each person sharing why they had decided to attend *Starting Point*. About halfway around the circle we came to a man named Randy, a rough looking big guy wearing a black leather jacket.

Leaning forward as if to challenge us, he declared with sincerity, "I have to be honest with you. I really don't care much for church people. I don't believe Jesus died on the cross or rose from the dead. I wouldn't be here today if my wife hadn't dragged me here. I came because I'm tired of listening to her nagging, but I probably won't be back next Sunday."

That's authenticity! I thanked Randy for sharing, and went on to the next person. After our group discussion ended that morning, I went over to Randy and thanked him again for coming to *Starting Point*.

He replied, "I normally have to work on Sundays, but I think I might try to rearrange my schedule so I can come back next Sunday."

Randy and his wife did come back that next Sunday, and the next. A few weeks later, Randy gave his life to Christ! Praise God!

The freedom to be authentic and honest without fear of judgment is the established norm for Christlike dialogue.

Randy and his wife Helen have become dear friends and supporters of *Christlike Dialogue*. At a recent ministry event Randy shared that the response he received in *Starting Point* was "unnatural". He hadn't expected to be warmly welcomed into a group of Christians who he thought would be judgmental and defensive of their beliefs because of his previous experience with "church people". Today Randy serves in a church ministry to poor and needy people. God has really transformed him!

4. **BE HUMBLE.** If one of the parties is in authority over the other(s), it's important to give people under authority freedom to respectfully discuss matters of concern without negative consequences.

"Jesus called them together and said, "You know that the rulers of the Gentiles lord it over them, and their high officials exercise authority over them. Not so with you. Instead, whoever wants to become great among you must be your servant, and whoever wants to be first must be your slave—just as the Son of Man did not come to be served, but to serve, and to give his life as a ransom for many" (Matthew 20:25-28).

The intent of this guideline is to grant the person under authority permission and freedom to share their concerns openly, without fear of being criticized or punished for it. Without this security, leadership would seldom learn how they and/

or their decisions impact those under their authority.

Many homes, churches and businesses operate far less efficiently and peacefully than possible when leadership fails to listen to the creative, beneficial ideas and insights that those under their authority are more than willing to share, if given the opportunity.

Leaders may also be unaware of certain personal weaknesses or character flaws that don't fit with their Christian testimony, which may be clearly evident to those around them, unless they give those under their authority permission to respectfully talk about these things openly with their leader in helpful, constructive, *iron sharpens iron* ways (Proverbs 27:17). The leader is then free to accept their comments as being true and helpful, or to reject them as being inaccurate, hopefully after giving prayerful consideration to what has been noted.

PUTTING CHRISTLIKE DIALOGUE INTO PRACTICE

When my sons, Rob and Travis, were growing up, I gave them the **freedom to confront** me when they thought I was wrong, as long as they did so **respectfully**. Once or twice a year, I would ask them, "What don't you like about me as a dad?" and "How can I be a better dad?"

My oldest son Rob once replied, "You're an over-thinker and an over-planner."

Impressed by my son's honest and accurate answer, I said, "Thank you, Rob. I am an over-thinker and an over-planner, so hopefully your reminder will help me loosen up and live a day at a time."

When my sons were home on summer vacation from college, one of God's greatest blessings was the privilege of working outdoors with them in our seasonal job of adjusting property insurance claims. We were a team and each of us had separate, supportive roles and responsibilities. One evening on our way home from a hard day's work, I asked again, "What don't you like about me as a dad?" and "How can I be a better dad?"

This time they respectfully implied that I was a controller and had not given them much say about their choice of roles while on the job. As they had several years of experience and did excellent work, that night I gave them the responsibility of deciding each person's role for the next day. I suggested that they choose their own assignments, assuming the role they felt most qualified to do and enjoyed the most. I also gave them permission to delegate the job assignment I should have. We thoroughly enjoyed that next day which turned out to be even more efficient than our previous arrangement.

YOUR TURN

If you are a person in authority over another, are you willing to give people under your authority the freedom to confront you, as long as they do so respectfully? If so, let them know that by asking them a question or two to initiate the dialogue. Here are two examples:

What weaknesses do you see in my life that are keeping me from being a godlier spouse, parent, employer, pastor, or friend?

What character qualities or habits of mine offend you, and what changes would you like to see in me that can improve our relationship?

Those are just examples. Prayerfully consider any questions you prefer to ask those who are under your authority.

5. **BE TEACHABLE.** Remain open to the possibility of being wrong about your position, and to the possibility of being deceived.

   "The heart is deceitful above all things and beyond cure. Who can understand it?" (Jeremiah 17:9).

   "If anyone considers himself religious and yet does not keep a tight rein on his tongue, he deceives himself and his religion is worthless" (James 1:26).

One day as I was riding in the car with my youngest son Travis, we had a little difference of opinion. As we talked, I began to realize he was right and I was wrong, so I said, "I was wrong, but…"

No sooner had the word "but" left my mouth, when Travis boldly replied, "Dad, no 'buts.' I just want to hear you say these three words, 'I was wrong.'"

I looked over at my son, smiled, and said, "Travis, I was wrong." I thanked him for holding me accountable as I had obviously tried to justify myself.

Those three words—**"I WAS WRONG"**—are powerful. They can restore marriages and keep churches from splitting. They can even prevent wars between countries. They have this effect only if people in authority are willing to say them with sincere humility. It's a matter of the heart.

If you allow others the freedom to confront you respectfully, you may become aware of personal weaknesses that can adversely affect the lives of others as well as your Christian witness. If that is the case, is there any reason not to welcome truth spoken in love?

6. **LISTEN.** Learn from one another and don't attempt to persuade others to your point of view or assume someone is wrong just because they don't agree with you. Seek to understand and be understood as to why each of you believes what you believe.

"My dear brothers, take note of this: Everyone should be quick to listen, slow to speak and slow to become angry, for man's anger does not bring about the righteous life that God desires" (James 1:19-20).

WHEN PEOPLE BARE THEIR SOULS to you, you are on holy ground. Your responsibility is to listen and love. if you jump in with both feet – trying to fix their problems – you pollute the holy terrain. Some people will retreat when this happens; others may be too wounded to realize they've been violated. Either way, you have spoiled a splendid opportunity.

To function effectively on holy ground, you need the help of the Holy Spirit. Ask Him to think through you, listen through you, love through you. As the Spirit's Love shines through you, My healing Presence goes to work in the other person. While you continue listening, your main role is to direct the person toward Me and My bountiful resources.

– Sarah Young, *Jesus Always*, p. 257

In Christlike dialogue, people with differing views share their personal life stories with one another and truly listen empathetically in order to learn from and better understand each other.

Sincere other-minded listening should be encouraged as each person answers the following questions as they relate to the issue or matter of concern at hand.

- What do you believe?
- Why do you believe that way?
- What is your source of truth that influenced your thinking?
- Do you believe that source of truth is reliable? Why or why not?

7. **PURSUE TRUTH.** Agree to give one another the freedom to speak the truth as each perceives it, without interruption from the other(s), except to ask questions for clarification. Agree to consider the Bible as a reliable source of truth and wisdom for life's challenges.

   Jesus said to him, "I am the way, and the truth, and the life..." (John 14:6, ESV).

   "And you will know the truth, and the truth will set you free" (John 8:32, ESV).

   "Behold, you delight in truth in the inward being, and you teach me wisdom in the secret heart" (Psalm 51:6, ESV).

8. **PERSEVERE IN LOVE.** It is not important to agree with one another; it is important

that you extend mutual respect and perfect courtesy to others, despite differences. This does not mean you condone something about which you disagree; but it does mean that you don't withdraw your love from others just because they don't see things exactly as you do. **Remember: the relationship is more important than the issue.**

"[Jesus said,] A new command I give you: Love one another. As I have loved you, so you must love one another. By this all men will know will know that you are my disciples, if you love one another" (John 13:34-35).

"Remind them to be submissive to rulers and authorities, to be obedient, to be ready for every good work, to speak evil of no one, to avoid quarreling, to be gentle, and to show perfect courtesy toward all people" (Titus 3:1-2, ESV).

REMEMBER: **The relationship is more important than the issue.**

9. **JUDGE NOT.** Refrain from being critical or judgmental of others.

"Do not judge, or you too will be judged. For in the same way you judge others, you will be judged, and with the measure you use, it will be measured to you.

"Why do you look at the speck of sawdust in your brother's eye and pay no attention to the plank in your own eye? How can you say to your brother, 'Let me take the speck out of your eye,' when all the time there is a plank in your own eye? You hypocrite, first take the plank out of your own eye, and then you will see clearly to remove the speck from your brother's eye" (Matthew 7:1-5).

Jesus' instructions in regard to judging others is very simply put; He says, "Don't." It is impossible to enter into fellowship with God when you are in a critical mood. Criticism serves to make you harsh, vindictive, and cruel, and leaves you with the soothing and flattering idea that you are somehow superior to others. You must constantly beware of anything that causes you to think of yourself as a superior person.
– Oswald Chambers, My Utmost for His Highest, June 17

A MEMORABLE MEETING

I once served as the program director for a prison ministry in Colorado. I interviewed prison inmates and I then interviewed Christians from various churches who were interested in meeting and building a friendship with one of the prison inmates. I then matched them up and introduced them to each other.

One day, as I was interviewing an inmate, he began to share his story. He told me he was a homosexual, dying from AIDS and went on to say that his father, an educated doctor, had frequently abused him. The abuse became so severe that at the age of twelve, social services placed the boy with foster care parents, a couple who claimed to be Christians. Later, as he began to experience some homosexual tendencies, the foster parents kicked him out of their home. Rejected by his dad, separated from both parents, and rejected by those he understood to be Christians, he explained that he was left alone to fend for himself. Then he shared these words with me, "Here I am, only in my thirties, a practicing homosexual, in prison, and dying from AIDS. But I want you to know that even though I have been rejected before, I'm willing to let you match me up with a Christian as long as they don't come here and tell me how bad I am, and that I need to change."

This young man was desperately in need of compassion and the loving-kindness of Jesus Christ, not a lecture.

10. **TRUST GOD WITH THE OUTCOME.** Agree to leave another person's decision, and the consequences of that decision, between that person and God. Some situations involving Christians may require church discipline to be administered in love.

   "When they hurled their insults at him, he did not retaliate; when he suffered, he made no threats. Instead, he entrusted himself to him who judges justly" (1 Peter 2:23).

   "And the Lord's servant must not quarrel; instead, he must be kind to everyone, able to teach, not resentful. Those who oppose him he must gently instruct, in the hope that God will grant them repentance leading them to a knowledge of the truth, and that they will come to their senses and escape from the trap of the devil, who has taken them captive to do his will" (2 Timothy 2:24-26).

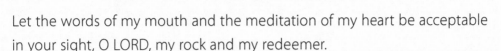

Let the words of my mouth and the meditation of my heart be acceptable in your sight, O LORD, my rock and my redeemer.

– Psalm 19:14, ESV

DISCUSSION QUESTIONS
CHAPTER 10

From Debate to Christlike Dialogue

1. Read and examine in detail the quote from The Miracle of Dialogue on page 117. What is your understanding of the significance of this quote if taken seriously?

2. Refer to the chart on page 118. Why do you think debate is more prevalent than Christlike dialogue? What specific impact could there be in our homes, churches, workplaces, and throughout society if Christlike dialogue became more prevalent than debates consisting of argumentative monologues?

3. For you personally, which of the *guidelines* is the most challenging to put into practice? Why?

4. What have you learned from this chapter and/or another part of this study that will equip you to represent Jesus well when engaging people with differing views in conversations that honor God?

GUIDELINE FOCUS:
TRUST GOD WITH THE OUTCOME

AGREE TO LEAVE ANOTHER PERSON'S DECISION, AND THE CONSEQUENCES OF THAT DECISION, BETWEEN THAT PERSON AND GOD. (1 PETER 2:23; 2 TIMOTHY 2:24-26) SOME SITUATIONS MAY REQUIRE CHURCH DISCIPLINE TO BE ADMINISTERED IN LOVE. (MATTHEW 18:15-17)

Look up 1 Peter 2:23 and 2 Timothy 2:24-26, the verses on which this guideline is based, and copy one of them into your Journal in Appendix B on page 145.

APPLICATION

As a pastor, I have witnessed firsthand the kind of destruction gossip, slander, and quarreling can produce among a church staff and congregation. It is devastating, and there are fewer things that bring greater reproach to the name of Christ. I have also experienced the power and love that comes through Christlike dialogue. There is heavenly quality and eternal weight that accompanies such love. This kind of love exalts Christ and makes him irresistible to the world. The struggle to attain Christlike love is a difficult one, but it is worth it!

This week, you're encouraged to ask the leadership at your church if they would prayerfully consider making Christlike dialogue a priority for your congregation and encourage all members to go through this study guide. Spend several months putting the principles into practice. Remind and encourage each other to replace gossip, quarreling, argumentative monologues, and all unkind and unloving words with conversations that honor God. As you put the principles into practice, set aside some time to share testimonies of lives being transformed through Christlike dialogue. Pray that your congregation will truly be known by your love for one another, even in the midst of conflict, for God's glory.

– Blake Burget
Evangelism Director
Prayer Director | Mission Hills Church

OUR PRAYER

As you conclude this study, our prayer is for each of you to know Christ better and to represent Him well through the words you speak (and don't speak) so others come to know Jesus for who He truly is. We pray that you are blessed and a blessing as you actively engage people with differing views in ways that honor God.

For God's Glory,
Jeff & Candy Rosenau
jr@ChristlikeDialogue.org / cr@ChristlikeDialogue.org

APPENDIX A GUIDELINES

1. **PRAY.** Ask God to help you gain a greater understanding of each other, of what is true, and of what God might want to reveal about himself through the conversation. (Psalm 18:30)

2. **FIND COMMON GROUND.** Identify a common subject of interset for the dialogue. Read John 4:1-26 for an example. It can be anything you can identify as common ground (such as water in the example) that might help you relate to one another more clearly.

3. **BE HONEST.** Authenticity is highly valued. (Proverbs 24:26)

4. **BE HUMBLE.** If one of the parties is in authority over the other(s), it's important to give people under authority freedom to respectfully discuss matters of concern without negative consequences. (Matthew 20:25-28)

5. **BE TEACHABLE.** Remain open to the possibility of being wrong about your position, and to the possibility of being deceived. (Proverbs 3:5-6; Jeremiah 17:9; James 1:26)

6. **LISTEN.** Learn from one another and don't attempt to persuade others to your point of view or assume someone is wrong just because he or she doesn't agree with you. Seek to understand and be understood as to why each of you believe what you believe. (James 1:19-20; Philippians 2:3-4)

7. **PURSUE TRUTH.** Agree to give one another the freedom to speak the truth as each perceives it, without interruption from the other(s), except to ask questions for clarification. Agree to consider the Bible as a reliable source of truth and wisdom for life's challenges. (Psalm 5:16; John 14:6, 8:32)

8. **PERSEVERE IN LOVE.** It is not important to agree with one another; it is important that you extend mutual respect and perfect courtesy to others, despite differences. This does not mean that you condone something about which you disagree; but it does mean that you don't withdraw your love from others just because they don't see things exactly as you do. Remember: the relationship is more important than the issue. (John 13:34-35; Titus 3:1-2)

9. **JUDGE NOT.** Refrain from being critical or judgemental of others. (Matthew 7:1-5)

10. **TRUST GOD WITH THE OUTCOME.** Agree to leave another person's decision, and the consequences of that decision, between that person and God. (1 Peter 2:23; 2 Timothy 2:24-26) Some situations may require church discipline to be administered in love. (Matthew 18:15-17)

APPENDIX B JOURNAL

CHAPTER 1: Jesus Didn't Die for us to Remain the Same

GUIDELINE FOCUS: PRAY

Write out Psalm 18:30 in the space provided:

Write out Psalm 19:14 in the space provided:

WEEKLY LOG

Jot down instances of negative speech and note the situation or person that provoked your response. Use the abbreviations: (G) Gossip, (Q) Quarrel, (D) Debate, (A) Apathy, (O) Other unkind, sarcastic, unloving words, and circle the letter that most applies.

EXAMPLE:

Sunday: G Q D A O *(circle one)*	
Words:	**Person/Situation:**
Yelling match about missing the school bus	Son's messy room

LOG FOR THE WEEK OF: _____

Sunday: G Q D A O *(circle one)*	
Words:	**Person/Situation:**
Morning:	
Afternoon:	
Evening:	

Monday: G Q D A O *(circle one)*	
Words:	**Person/Situation:**
Morning:	
Afternoon:	
Evening:	

Tuesday: G Q D A O *(circle one)*	
Words:	**Person/Situation:**
Morning:	
Afternoon:	
Evening:	

Wednesday: G Q D A O *(circle one)*

Words:	Person/Situation:
Morning:	
Afternoon:	
Evening:	

Thursday: G Q D A O *(circle one)*

Words:	Person/Situation:
Morning:	
Afternoon:	
Evening:	

Friday: G Q D A O *(circle one)*

Words:	Person/Situation:
Morning:	
Afternoon:	
Evening:	

Saturday: G Q D A O *(circle one)*	
Words:	**Person/Situation:**
Morning:	
Afternoon:	
Evening:	

Patterns Observed this Week:

GUIDELINE FOCUS: BE HONEST

Write out Proverbs 24:26 in the space provided.

Write out Psalm 139:23-24 in the space provided.

Write out Ephesians 4:29-32 in the space provided.

This week write a letter to ask for forgiveness for some specific 'unwholesome talk' or offensive, hurtful, or harsh words you may have spoken or tone/inflection you may have used.

GUIDELINE FOCUS: LISTEN

Write out James 1:19-20 in the space provided.

Write out Philippians 2:3-4 in the space provided.

In the space provided, list the qualities of effective listening. Use your list from question 2 and any additional insights you gained from your group's discussion time. Circle the top three qualities that you will focus on improving in the weeks ahead.

Qualities of Effective Listening

GUIDELINE FOCUS: JUDGE NOT

Write out Matthew 7:1-5 in the space provided.

Write out Romans 2:1 in the space provided.

Ask God to show you how He might want you to **seize the opportunity to speak the truth in love** in a tangible way to a person or group of people who have a very different viewpoint than you on a particular issue. Perhaps it is a social or political issue, or a group of people you have stereotyped, or for you perhaps it is the person whose name you wrote down in Chapter Two that you are struggling to forgive.

Use this space to write out a prayer to God to ask Him how He would like you to proceed. You might also share your situation and seek the prayers from other(s) in your group.

After praying, use this space to write down the action steps you will take.

GUIDELINE FOCUS: BE TEACHABLE

Look up Proverbs 3:5-6, Jeremiah 17:9, and James 1:26, and write out one or two of them in the space provided. Choose one to memorize.

After spending an hour in prayer to prepare your heart for dialogue, if God is leading you to, schedule a time to dialogue with someone you have identified through your quiet time. Also, look back at Chapter 1, question 5 on page 14 and your Journal entry for Chapter 2 on p. 135.

Use the Guidelines found on page 130 for dialogue. Record what God revealed to you through the dialogue in the space below.

GUIDELINE FOCUS: PURSUE TRUTH

Write out Psalm 51:6 in the space provided.

Write out John 14:6 in the space provided.

Write out John 8:32 in the space provided.

Choose one of the previous three verses to memorize.

List names of non-Christians who God has laid on your heart to pray for:

Use the template provided in Appendix C on pages 146-147 to prepare "your story". Christians use the term, "testimony", but "your story" might be better when talking with someone who is not yet a Christian. Once you have prepared your story, copy your notes in the space below and be prepared to practice telling it to your group. Aim for 3 minutes.

Before I Accepted Christ

How I Received Christ

After I Became a Follower of Jesus Christ

GUIDELINE FOCUS: FIND COMMON GROUND

What is the definition of *Christlike Dialogue*?

_____

(Philippians 2:3-4; James 1:19-20)

_____

(John 14:6; 8:32; Ephesians 4:15)

_____

(1 Timothy 1:15; Ephesians 4:13)

_____

(1 Peter 2:23; 2 Timothy 2:24-26)

I choose to engage in conversation with my non-believing friend or acquaintance,

_____

about who Jesus is. One area of common ground for us is:

_____

To prepare for the conversation, first pray; then review the suggested questions from Chapters 6 and 7 as well as your testimony.

After the conversation, use the space below to record what you learned through this experience. Include the emotions you experienced.

GUIDELINE FOCUS: BE HUMBLE

Write out Matthew 20:25-28 in the space provided.

Humble/meek people display the following characteristics:

Read Genesis 1:27 and James 3:9-10 and then paraphrase them in your own words and write them in the space provided; then, compose a prayer from these verses, asking God to forgive you for past offensive words you have used to speak of people made in the image of God. Ask Him to give you the ability and desire to see others through Jesus' eyes. If God specifically brings to mind a person or group of people you have stereotyped or gossiped about, include that in your prayer.

Genesis 1:27

James 3:9-10

Lord, I pray

CHAPTER 9: Persevere in Love, Despite Differences

GUIDELINE FOCUS: PERSEVERE IN LOVE

Write out John 13:34-35 in the space provided.

Write out Titus 3:1-2 in the space provided.

I will persevere in love with others despite differences by taking the following action steps:

GUIDELINE FOCUS: TRUST GOD WITH THE OUTCOME

Write out 1 Peter 2:23 in the space provided.

Write out 2 Timothy 2:24-26 in the space provided and underline the 3 "musts".

Write out Matthew 18:15-17 in the space provided. (To learn about church discipline, if needed.)

APPENDIX C: TESTIMONY TEMPLATE

How to Share My Testimony – adopted from Campus Crusade for Christ International; https://www.cru.org/train-and-grow/share-the-gospel/evangelism-principles/how-to-tell-your-story-worksheet.html#

ANSWER THESE QUESTIONS:

Before I Accepted Christ (or gave Him complete control)

1. What was my life like that will relate most to the non-Christian?

2. What did my life revolve around the most? What did I get my security or happiness from?

3. How did those areas begin to let me down?

How I Received Christ (or gave Him complete control)

1. When was the first time I heard the gospel?

2. What were my initial reactions?

3. When did my attitude begin to turn around? Why?

4. What were the final struggles that went through my mind just before I accepted Christ?

5. Why did I go ahead and accept Christ?

After I Accepted Christ (or gave Him complete control)

1. Specific changes and illustrations about the changes Christ has made:

2. Why am I motivated differently?

Helpful Hints

1. Write the way you speak; make the testimony yours.
2. Practice this over and over until it becomes natural.
3. Shoot for short -- 3 minutes. At that length, it's easily something you can put into a conversation without it becoming a monologue.

An example: Look at Paul's testimony as you consider how to tell your story.

His life before (Acts 22:1-5) Paul describes what he thought and did before he became a believer.

Your goal: to give specific, yet appropriate, examples of what your life was like (attitudes, needs, problems) before Christ. Remember that examples you give will establish you as a credible witness in the minds of non-Christians. However, avoid a religious focus. (You want to make it about Jesus and your need for Him.) Don't spend a great amount of time talking about church activities or denominations before your life began to change. Likewise, avoid being explicit and sensational in speaking of drugs, immorality, crime or drunkenness.

How (Acts 22:6-11) Paul explained how he became a believer.

Your goal: to allow the listener to walk away with a clear understanding of how you became a Christian and how he or she can trust Christ as the payment for their sins. Be careful not to use clichés and church language. Talk in terms they'll understand.

After (Acts 22:12-21) Paul explained how becoming a believer changed his life.

Your goal: to explain specific ways Christ has changed your life -- to show that having Christ in your life really does make a difference!
   Avoid using general statements such as "I have so much peace now." Be specific. It is the Holy Spirit's responsibility to draw someone to Christ, but you want to communicate your story in such a way to show the listener that your life is different and more meaningful with Christ.

ENDNOTES

The following are the sources of excerpts used in this book:

Chapter 1: JESUS DIDN'T DIE FOR US TO REMAIN THE SAME

1. Billy Graham, *The Journey* (Nashville, TN: W Publishing Group, a division of Thomas Nelson, Inc., 2006), 78-79.

Chapter 2: SEIZE THE OPPORTUNITY

2. W. Glyn Evans, *Daily with my Lord* (Chicago, IL: The Moody Bible Institute, 1999), August 20.

Chapter 3: OTHER-MINDED LISTENING

3. John Vawter, Uncommon Graces (Colorado Springs, CO: NavPress, 1998), 44-45, 56.

4. Emerson Eggerichs, *Love & Respect: The Love She Most Desires, the Respect He Desperately Needs.* (Nashville, TN: Thomas Nelson, 2004), 6.

5. Garry Poole, *The Complete Book of Questions: 1001 Conversation Starters for Any Occasion.* (Poole, 2003).

Chapter 4: SEEK AND SPEAK THE TRUTH IN LOVE

6. Paul David Tripp, *War of Words: Getting to the Heart of Your Communication Struggles* (Phillipsburg, NJ: P&R Publishing Company, 2000), 7.

Chapter 5: GRACE, TRUTH, AND TOLERANCE

7. Randy Alcorn, *The Grace and Truth Paradox* (Sisters, OR: Multnomah Publishers, Inc., 2003), 18, 20, 87, 92.

8. Andrew Murray, *Abiding in Christ* (Bloomington, MN: Bethany House Publishers, 2003), 122.

9. Sam Allberry, *Is God Anti-Gay?: and other questions about homosexuality, the Bible and same-sex attraction.* (Purcellville, VA: The Good Book Company, 2015).

Chapter 6: FOCUS ON CHRIST'S INTERESTS

10. Augustine

Chapter 7: TRUST GOD WITH THE OUTCOME

11. Roy Hession, *The Calvary Road* (London: Christian Literature Crusade, 1950), 98-101.

Chapter 8: THE MEEK SURRENDER, BUT NEVER LOSE

12. Richard A. Swenson, M.D., *Margin* (Colorado Springs, CO: NavPress, 1992), 233-234.

13. Oxford University Press, Inc., *Oxford American Dictionary* (New York, NY: Oxford University Press, 1980), 32, 547.

Chapter 9: PERSEVERE IN LOVE, DESPITE DIFFERENCES

14. Heath Lambert, November 7, 2016 edition of *Truth in Love*

15. Martin Luther King, Jr., August 16, 1967, *"Where Do We Go From Here?"*, delivered at the 11th Annual Southern Christian Leadership Conference in Atlanta, GA.

Chapter 10: FROM DEBATE TO CHRISTLIKE DIALOGUE

16. Reuel L. Howe, *The Miracle of Dialogue* (Minneapolis, MN: The Seabury Press, Incorporated, 1963), 3-4.

17. Sarah Young, *Jesus Always: Embracing Joy in His Presence* (Nashville, TN: Thomas Nelson, 2016), 257.

18. Oswald Chambers, *My Utmost for His Highest* (Grand Rapids, MI: Discovery House Publishers, 1992), June 17.

CPSIA information can be obtained
at www.ICGtesting.com
Printed in the USA
JSHW020731140819
1080JS00001BA/2